POEMS ARE TEACHERS

How Studying Poetry Strengthens Writing in All Genres

AMY LUDWIG VANDERWATER

HEINEMANN
Portsmouth, NH

Heinemann
361 Hanover Street
Portsmouth, NH 03801–3912
www.heinemann.com

Offices and agents throughout the world

The author and publisher wish to thank those who have generously given permission to reprint borrowed material:

"Riches" by Mary Lee Hahn. Copyright © 2018 by Mary Lee Hahn. Used with permission from the author.

Acknowledgments for borrowed material continue on page 243.

Library of Congress Cataloging-in-Publication Data
Names: VanDerwater, Amy Ludwig, author.
Title: Poems are teachers : how studying poetry strengthens writing in all genres / Amy Ludwig VanDerwater.
Description: Portsmouth, NH : Heinemann, 2017. | Includes bibliographical references.
Identifiers: LCCN 2017022511 | ISBN 9780325096537
Subjects: LCSH: Poetry—Study and teaching. | Poetry—Authorship.
Classification: LCC PN1101 .V36 2017 | DDC 808.1/07—dc23

LC record available at https://lccn.loc.gov/2017022511

Editor: Katie Wood Ray
Production: Vicki Kasabian
Cover and interior designs: Suzanne Heiser
Cover image: Getty Images
Author photograph: Melissa Deakin Photography
Typesetter: Kim Arney
Manufacturing: Steve Bernier

Printed in the United States of America on acid-free paper
21 20 19 18 17   RWP   1 2 3 4 5

FOR LEE BENNETT HOPKINS,

WHO FILLS THE WORLD WITH POETRY AND LAUGHTER

CONTENTS

4 Writers Play with Language 121
Learn to Play with Language from Poems

Foreword

Amy's grand title, *Poems Are Teachers: How Studying Poetry Strengthens Writing in All Genres*, names the promise of this book, and every ravishing word thereafter supports that thesis and never lets us down. Amy convinces us that devoting time to deep study and practice of the specific features and techniques of poetry will elevate any type of prose, and we should determine to make plenty of space for poem reading and writing in our classrooms.

Amy's prolific practice as a writer of jewel-like poems certainly gives her authority to pronounce poetry as teacher of all kinds of writing. Witness this very book as proof! The prose sings; the ideas enthrall; the organization invigorates. Amy's writing is like a Dove Chocolate—elegant and unassuming, but oh, so rich. Her language illuminates and delights, as in this sentence: "But remember, like chefs, writers are creative people, and they often invent new ways to combine phrase-ingredients and word-spices" (123). Or this one: "Our hearts have been zipped open with words" (187). Writing that delicious inspires me to produce a bumper sticker, or indeed, a national standard that will apply in every classroom for every age group: *Teach poetry writing because poetry teaches everything*.

I can attest to Amy's claim that the art and skill of making poems strengthens all kinds of composition. Writing poetry, I often joke, helped earn my college degrees. My course papers stood out in the stacks of essays and gave my professors some joy to read, or so they reported. I believe the techniques I learned making poems translated to my prose writing, affecting everything from provocative titles, to sentence cadence and variety, and especially to lessons in revising (cutting, mostly) for clarity and meaning. Astronomy class? Over my head, much of it, and I made a C on the multiple-choice exam. But my research paper contained a galaxy of metaphors, and in a sort of bonus section, I included several poems, one that compared the end of an unfortunate love relationship to a supernova explosion, where one of the stars steals matter from its companion star, exhausting its nuclear fuel. (Or something like that.) Perhaps the poem's metaphor demonstrated for my professor that I had a reasonable understanding of the science.

Unlike the murkiness of my supernova–love analogy, the organization of this book is crystal clear and effective. You can dip in and out as you wish, in any order you prefer, to find a lesson that teaches an art or a technique of poem writing. The teaching comes in the form of quick try-its that will fly out of the book and into kids' hearts, inviting them to write poems with strength, wit, and beauty.

You can also keep this book open on your desk as a constant companion to consult for powerful lessons in crafting fiction, essay, and argument writing, or for sparking informational texts during science, history, and math. Amy provides numerous examples of poetic techniques inside all kinds of narrative and nonnarrative prose texts that you can use to demonstrate.

As if the wealth of Amy's own writing and teaching ideas were not enough by themselves, she gifts us with a trove of poems by our favorite children's poets, who reveal the secrets of their thinking and their craft decisions for each contribution. Jane Yolen's explanation of the multiple reasons she chose the word *smudge* is priceless. In addition, Amy presents dozens of stunning poems by young students working with the various poetry techniques that sit companionably beside their mentors.

I promise that you are about to experience joy reading this book. I am positive that sharing the poems, the how-tos, and the inner workings of all these poets' hearts and minds with your students will magically, even miraculously improve their poetry and prose. And I hope that some of Amy Ludwig VanDerwater's magic dust will inspire you to write your own poems as well.

—Katherine Bomer

ACKNOWLEDGMENTS

My deepest gratitude to . . .

The many writing teachers and authors who have guided and continue to guide my thinking with your workshops and books. Thank you, Lucy Calkins, for beginning my journey. And thank you to everyone in that Teachers College office back in the early '90s. I still look up to you all. Thank you, Carl Anderson, for breaking down professional book writing for me ages ago. It took a long time, but I listened.

Poets. Thank you to all of you, those I've met and those I've never met. You enrich life. Special thank-yous to the Poetry Friday community and to all poets, of all ages, who share poems in these pages. Your voices make this book sing.

Teachers and friends. Thank you for welcoming me into your nurturing classrooms, in 3-D life and through *The Poem Farm*. Extra special gratitude to all of you who connected me with the students whose work appears in this book: Helene Albrecht, Heidi Ames, Jenn Bogard, Ashlee Bryant, Cathi Burton, Emily Callahan, Susan Chauncey, Winifred Christopher, Andria Nacina Cole, Ann Marie Corgill, Monica Crudele, Darlene Daley, Mali Dayton, Kim Doele, Debbi Dolce, Michelle Enser, Ketty Fernandez, Catherine Flynn, Michele Gilbert-Tindall, Mona Goodman, Charnetta Harvey, Keith Hinnant, Nicole Jamison, Jessica Ketcheson, Pam Koutrakos, Barry Lane, Nancy Logghe, JoEllen McCarthy, Patty McGee, Alicia McKenrick, Melanie Meehan, Kimberley Moran, Karen Morreale, Kim Oldenburgh, Brianna Peros, Ann Piper, Tia Rendine, Mary Anne Sacco, Christine Scheer, Margaret Simon, Tara Smith, Kathleen Sokolowski, Angela Stockman, Holly VanEpps, Darren Victory, Aliza Werner, and David Williams.

Elizabeth Harding, my wise agent at Curtis Brown Ltd. You know best, and I am lucky to have your knowledgeable and encouraging voice in my head and heart.

My dear, smart, kind friends, especially Karen Caine, my forever writing pal and funny poet.

Katherine Bomer, the big sister I wish I had, for teaching me by example and for your ever-generous foreword.

My loving family. Thank you to my parents George and Debby, my sister Heidi, my in-laws Bruce and Betty, and all of my sisters and brothers in-law. You are very kind to listen to these book stories. Thank you especially to Mark, Hope, Georgia, and Henry, my loves. And extra gratitude to Georgia, for sweeping in with a light heart and a willingness to help with poem organization and permissions.

The powerful and gracious team at Heinemann. A book only becomes a book with a team. Thank you to editorial coordinator and permissions getter Edie Davis Quinn, senior permissions specialist Maria Czop, cover and text designer Suzanne Heiser, freelance copy editor Jennifer Brett Greenstein, marketing product manager Kim Cahill, manufacturing print buyer Steve Bernier, production director Patty Adams, senior production editor Vicki Kasabian, and every person at Heinemann who touched this book even for a second. I thank you for your expertise and, too, for your kindness.

My friend and acquisitions editor Katie Wood Ray, who taught me to read again with her book *Wondrous Words* and who taught me to write again with her brilliant, patient, good-humored editing prowess. You are a model editor.

Lee Bennett Hopkins, my teacher to whom this book is dedicated. Thank you for believing in all of us.

Every single human who makes time for poems—you light the path.

Thank you
Thank you for
— beautiful sunsets
— swiming dolphins
Thank you for
— screeching egls
— my sister being quiet
Thank you for
— fresh kale
— sweet rass bares
Thank you for
— soft dogs
— sheeps fur
by Tucker B.
Grade 2

INTRODUCTION

Why Poems?

Poems are teachers. From grandparents' lullabies to rhyming picture books to barroom limericks to long-remembered eulogies, we all have ribbons of poetry tied to our bones. Poems change us. Anyone lucky enough to have been read poetry as a child carries certain lines forever, and anyone who has found poetry as an adult knows to hang on as if to a wild horse. For poems wake us up, keep us company, remind us that our world is big and small. And, too, poems teach us how to write. Anything.

Poems are the words of people who long to tell stories, teach, invite thoughts. Poems are shaped differently than prose, but reading poetry closely is a smart way to explore the qualities of *all* strong writing, from meaning to organization. From poetry, we learn to:

- find ideas and self-inspire

- structure texts

- use language in pleasing and surprising ways

- craft beginnings and endings

- choose titles

Poems Are Teachers is a book about learning how to write well by studying poems. Writers of all genres must have ideas, must organize these thoughts, must hammer interesting phrases together, must begin and end, must title. Poets arrange words and phrases just as prose writers do, simply in tighter spaces. In the tight space of poetry, readers can identify writing techniques after reading one page, not thirty pages. We notice how a poet writes with sensory imagery, and the very next morning we open the newspaper to find an opinion columnist using this same technique. Same tool, different genre. Beginning with poems, we can teach students to recognize craft and deepen their understandings of it across genres and beyond specific assignments.

My Poetry Connection

I still have my childhood copy of Gyo Fujikawa's *A Child's Book of Poems*, and I now own the little three-ring binder of poems that my great-aunt Tom (the flapper) typed for herself. I remember Professor O'Brien's voice as he read us Theodore Roethke's "My Papa's Waltz" in the basement at SUNY Geneseo so many years ago, and today, when I feel joyous or lost, I try to find a poem to match my mood. I am grateful for others' words; poems have made me me.

I write poems too. From April 2010 to April 2011, I wrote and shared a poem and poetry minilesson every day at my blog, *The Poem Farm*. Waiting for *Forest Has a Song* to be published, I spent April 2010 posting a new poem every day for National Poetry Month and came to appreciate the daily practice of finding an idea, structuring a text, playing with words, and publishing, all within twenty-four hours. The practice was so interesting that I continued posting fresh daily poems for 365 days. That year taught me a lot about writing.

My experience as a fifth-grade teacher, writing teacher, and author of essays and children's books has taught me, over and over, that poetry is our wisest writing teacher. Through the short lines of a poem, we can explore everything from the joy of rhythm to how print layout changes a reader's pace. We fall to our knees in wonder at the beauty of words, and then we dust off those same knees and get to work strengthening our own sentences.

Putting This Book to Work

By looking at the following chart, you will see how various respected writing teachers describe strong writing with different words but much the same meaning.

STRONG WRITING CHART

6 + 1 Traits of Writing Education Northwest educationnorthwest.org	*Teaching the Qualities of Writing* JoAnn Portalupi and Ralph Fletcher	*Assessing Writers* Carl Anderson	**Use this column to** • plan a unit • study a poem or other text • look at student writing
Ideas	Content	Meaning	
Organization	Design	Structure	
Word Choice	Language	Detail	
Sentence Fluency			
Conventions	Presentation	Conventions	
Presentation			
Voice	Voice	Voice	

As writing teachers, our work is to help students understand how the qualities of strong writing transcend genre, and for me that work has been grounded in this chart. Not comfortable with seeing things in only one way, I pieced the columns together from the wise work of the *6 + 1 Traits* researchers at Education Northwest (see also Culham 2016), and JoAnn Portalupi and Ralph Fletcher (2004), and Carl Anderson (2005). This chart lives inside my writing teacher mind. Whenever I read students' writing, I listen to ideas/content/meaning first. Is this writing meaningful to writer and reader? Does it make sense? Then I move to organization/design/structure, considering the way the text is sewn together. Can a reader follow it? How do the pieces fit? How does the work begin and end? If it is well organized, I move to language, noting clever turns of phrase, metaphor, fresh descriptions. Lastly, I study grammar and conventions. Voice, for me, is the way a writer juggles these qualities of strong writing balls, the style with which she keeps them in the air. The blank column is where I might take conferring notes about a particular writer or plan lessons for a certain genre, using these qualities of writing as a planning guide.

In this book, you will explore the qualities of strong writing through the craft of particular poems. Depending on your needs and interests, there are many ways you might choose to use this resource, but whichever you choose, please enjoy the poems first. Read aloud together. Read quietly. Sketch or paint a line from a poem. Act out a poem. Play with words and reread. Share a poem each morning or week, collecting favorite lines. Make time to read and fall in love with texts—before you study craft. See, when we as readers care about the words of a poem, we will be interested in learning how the writer moved us. We must fall in love first.

Here are a few possible ways you might use this book.

TECHNIQUE OF THE WEEK IN WRITERS' NOTEBOOKS

Many young writers in grades 3 and up keep notebooks focused on a current genre of study. But writers' notebooks are the perfect place to experiment with new writing moves outside of genre study. Sharing techniques from this book during notebook time is one way to breathe life into your students' notebooks. Share one of the explorations in this book and give students a few minutes to try out the technique, either with an old entry or with a new one.

You might anchor students' study of craft in a "Technique of the Week," grounded in poetry but then expanded out to other genres. For example, students might study circular endings with Rebecca Kai Dotlich's poem "Cabin of One Hundred Lights" on Monday, add this technique to their palettes, experiment with it in their notebooks, and throughout the week notice and collect circular beginnings and endings from information, narrative, and opinion texts. Keeping track of these techniques in writers' notebooks, in a collective class craft notebook (a place to keep track of class learnings about craft), or on charts will help students develop repertoires across genres.

LESSONS AND MENTORS IN CURRENT UNITS AND CONFERENCES

If you're looking for mentor texts or language to help explain a particular writing technique, use this book to add a lesson to an existing writing unit, showing students how they might end articles with a brief word or phrase or find essay ideas by studying artwork. Similarly, as students draft and revise, use this book during writing conferences, sharing model poems by contemporary poets and children as you teach students new techniques. Make sure it's clear that the strong writing students admire in poems translates directly to the strong writing they admire in other genres.

A POETRY UNIT

You might use this book to plan a unit of poetry. Choose a few lessons from each chapter to tailor a monthlong or mini poetry unit, and use the mentor texts provided. If you do this, be sure to check out the books and visit the websites of the poets highlighted. The world of poetry for children is vast and beautiful, including yet extending far beyond humor and acrostics.

About the Poems

Each exploration in this book includes three poems, one by a contemporary adult poet and two by students. Be sure to share the quotes from the contemporary poets with your students, and invite them to explore the highlighted poetry books and websites to find new favorites.

While I have selected poems as models for each technique in this book, both for ease of use and to introduce readers to new poets, feel free to use your own favorites or to collect additional poems for each technique. The poems here are possible models, but I imagine teachers and students keeping classroom scrapbooks of techniques, including examples of poetry and prose that highlight each type of craft. Such scrapbooks might include a mishmash of poets, from a famous poet to a second grader who just wrote his first list poem.

The student poems may more closely match the style of poems your own students will write, so be sure to share these. Rhyme is difficult to master, and in order to highlight meaning and focus on various poetic techniques, most student poems in this book do not rhyme. Rather, these students have closely attended to literary techniques such as point of view, repetition, and onomatopoeia.

It was difficult to decide where to place many poems in this book, as each one demonstrates a variety of interesting writing moves. Talk with your students about anything they notice and admire in any poem you read together. After all, each poem can teach many writing techniques. For example, a poem might tell a story *and* use a simile *and* have a mysterious title.

Should you wish to share any of your students' poems with me, please contact me through my website, www.amyludwigvanderwater.com. I keep a catalog of student poems, by technique, at *The Poem Farm*, as a reference for teachers and young writers, and I welcome new poetry.

Finally, I encourage you to keep the same type of notebook or folder that your students keep as you explore these poems and techniques together. When teachers experiment with new writing tools, they understand those tools more deeply, and a notebook is a safe place to jump into new strategies, to take risks. When you write with your students, you become a true part of your classroom writing community. You can say, "When I tried this . . ." and students will learn from you, the writer-teacher who shares their journey.

My Hope

In February 2015, I had the good fortune to visit Wealthy Elementary School in East Grand Rapids, Michigan. There, in the voice of the state of Alaska, third-grade Hayden invited readers of his poem to "Let your huskies roam and rumble."

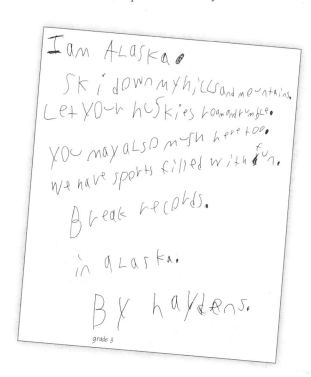

grade 3

Hayden's line made me smile, and I can still see those huskies, roaming, rumbling in the cold. My wish for you, Reader, is that the huskies of word and line and stanza will rumble you joyfully through the snowy hills of poetry. May these huskies of word and line and stanza show you that poetry—the heart and craft of it—is everywhere, in our lives, in our magazines, in our newspapers, and in our souls.

xo,
a.

1
....

WRITERS FIND IDEAS

What shall I write about? Where do ideas come from? Before experimenting with organizational structures and fine-tuning metaphors, a writer must begin with a spark, a story, a message. And this is where our teaching about how to write becomes teaching about how to live, how to pay attention, how to pull a rabbit-of-writing out of the hat-of-daily-life.

When planning to build a house, you begin with a dream. You desire a home with lots of light or a warm, open kitchen. You know what you want this home to give you, your family, your guests. Well, a writer, too, has a dream. This dream is to make a reader cry or laugh, connect to new information, or see something in a new way. And just as a prospective home builder begins with limitless possibilities, a writer starts with all possibilities. Sometimes, though, when given too many choices, we become paralyzed. "Write about anything" can easily become "I have nothing to write about." As a person who prefers menus with three choices to those with three hundred, I understand this struggle.

Many students are unaccustomed to discovering their own writing subjects. Year after year, when a child is required to write about holidays or to cite textual evidence at every turn, she might forget that she once rescued a worm at the bus stop, might forget that he is enchanted by sign language and frightened by German shepherds. To develop confidence in selecting ideas, a writer needs instruction in ways to choose ideas: You might try this; you might try that. You might even just look around, might just let an idea surprise you.

Drawing

I pick up my pencil
Ready to draw
But wait
I don't know
What to do
I look around
I look
And look
I can't find anything
But then
Here comes a butterfly
Comeing to me
Here I go
Drawing its wings

By: Emily
Grade 3

Our students can become magicians of words, pulling idea-rabbits out of their lives, but idea-finding takes practice. Students need a variety of ways to choose writing topics and time to discover which are most helpful. Just as sports require warm-ups, writing exercises can warm up students' minds.

I believe we should offer students many ways to discover ideas and, too, offer them practice in forced inspiration: keeping notebooks, arranging treasures on desks, collecting quotes, setting timers. We can give our students practice in developing such habits when we explain, "Today we will try an idea-finding strategy. It may work for you; it may not. Either way, you will have a new strategy to try when you are staring at blank paper. And throughout your lives, different strategies may work better at different times."

Learn to Find Writing Ideas from Poems

Because poems are usually short, we can study a pile of poems and walk away with many new ways to find writing ideas. We can do what Katie Wood Ray taught us in *What You Know by Heart* (2002), imagining the "office work" of any poet. We may not know exactly how a poet found an idea for a poem, but we can guess. We can ask our students, "How *do you think* this poet found the idea for this poem? *Perhaps* he was reading a book, and the book gave him the idea. *Maybe* the poet visited a museum and was struck by a piece of art. *It could be that* the poet was remembering his childhood." Questions such as these teach students an important habit of mind, to think about where ideas come from and to imagine possibilities from their own lives. When we ask these questions, we hang a challenge in the air: "Hey, we could find ideas this same way. Let's try it right now."

Discovering ideas in a variety of ways, finding inspiration in different places, is similar to content development in other genres. For example, a student writing about immigration might write from facts to develop content, but she might also respond to photographs, write in the voice of an immigrant, and interview immigration experts.

To help students study idea finding, look through a one-author poetry collection, discussing the possible inspirations for each poem. This will inform poetry writing, but also idea finding in other genres. Rather than inviting students to write a poem about horses after reading a poem about horses, we can get behind the horse-finding idea, encouraging students to find ideas (not copy topics) in the ways their favorite poets do.

Enjoy these poems and inspiration ideas, remembering that idea-finding techniques can help inspire your students in any genre.

Riches

I never met anyone
who found as many coins as you.
Sometimes it seemed
they had been left deliberately
knowing you'd be along soon
to scoop them up.

I came to realize
you were simply more aware,
also spotting hawks
IDing trees
and sighting lightning bugs
before I knew they were there.

Even as we walked through the ruined garden
after the first hard freeze
you found beauty,
lifting a disk of ice
from the bird bath
inviting light to spill through.

—*Mary Lee Hahn*

Ice from the Birdbath © 2010 by Mary Lee Hahn

WORDS FROM THE POET

My process for writing "Riches" started with browsing through all my photos, looking for one that "spoke" to me. My photos are my visual writer's notebook. Each picture could be the seed idea for a piece of writing. When I choose a photo, I notice everything in it. Then I think about who or what might be just outside the edges of the photo. I stay open to surprises. . . . The poems I write may bear little or no resemblance to the photo I have chosen. The ice in this photo looked like a giant coin, and I was thinking of that part in Annie Dillard's Pilgrim at Tinker Creek *that starts with her childhood obsession with hiding pennies and then goes on to detail all different ways of seeing. I was also thinking about the way my husband AJ actually sees (and avoids) screws and nails in the street and on roads when he's driving. The person speaking in this poem could sometimes be me talking about AJ, or it could be him talking about me. We are both noticers.*

CONSIDER THE TECHNIQUE

I remember sitting in the auditorium at Teachers College, Columbia University, over twenty years ago, writing with hundreds of teachers, accepting an invitation to "write from a photograph." We could choose a photograph we had on us, or a photograph we knew existed, or even a photograph that "never was, but should have been taken." This is an exercise I have returned to many times.

Writing in all genres can start with photographs. Photos are windows through which we see into different times, cultures, and lives. Photographs inspire news stories, and magazines such as *National Geographic* are famous for pairing photos with feature and travel articles. Photographer and media activist Mahmoud Raslan's 2016 photograph of Omran Daqneesh, the injured five-year-old Syrian child, inspired six-year-old Alex from New York to write a letter to President Obama inviting Omran to live with him (Chappell 2016). Photographs beget writing.

Students might write about photographs from their own lives, learning from Mary Lee Hahn who says, "My photos are my visual writer's notebook." Students might take photos and keep them as writing inspiration, pasting them into notebooks, writing around the edges. And for students who know photos only from cell phones, we can share hardcover memoirs and scrapbooks, showing how people write notes and stories about pictures, to remember their lives, to remember what was.

Students can study photographs taken by others: historical photographs, pictures from magazines or newspapers, artistic photographs, old pictures of strangers found at estate sales. Have you seen how some people have turned these into humorous greeting cards, imagining the captions? In this way, an old piece of photographic art becomes a new one, recycled and given fresh life.

A Few Places to Find Photos for Writing Inspiration

- home

- magazines

- estate and garage gales

- Library of Congress Prints and Photographs Online Catalog

- *National Geographic*'s "Photography" page online

A Few Poetry Collections Inspired by Photographs

- *Something Permanent* by Cynthia Rylant

- *Color Me a Rhyme*; and *Once Upon Ice* by Jane Yolen

- *Birmingham, 1963* and *Remember the Bridge: Poems of a People* by Carole Boston Weatherford

TRY IT

Photographs provide an endless well of inspiration. To begin, you may write lists from photos. Try a T-chart with everyone looking at the same photo for a few minutes: "What I See / What I Think . . . Wonder . . . Feel . . . Know." Talk about how differently students approach the same photograph. Then invite everyone to write from different photographs.

Encourage students to write from photos during social studies or science, taking on roles and making new connections from pictures. Students might make lists of questions, memories, or words that come to mind when studying a photo, or think about the meaning a picture holds and freewrite from their first thoughts. Remind them how Mary Lee Hahn notices everything in a photo, thinks about what might be just outside the edges, and stays open for surprises. To "stay open" is an important—and sometimes challenging—skill for a writer.

Regardless of how students write from photos, help them understand that freewrites and jottings from photographs can become longer drafts of nonfiction, opinion, narrative, and poetry too.

The Spark of Resurgence by Nathan Johnson

Veins of the sky

Its favorite victims
are sky scrapers
the veins of the sky
strike us
if we live
we are marked forever
from the veins of the sky

BY Isaiah T
grade 4

When I Was a Boy

When I was a boy
My grandpa had a boat
A large boat; on a dock; with a crow's
nest atop.

When I was a boy
I would climb atop it with my telescope
I loved that boat.

When I was a boy
I sat on the grey cushioned seat
Looking up at the stars;

When I was a boy
sitting atop that crow's nest
I had the time of my life.

by Sam
grade 4

Vero Beach © 2010 by Heidi Ames

A Dream of Wheat

After Green Wheat Fields, Auvers,
by Vincent van Gogh

From a plain
packet of seeds

comes sun-
sweetened stalks

seasoned by wind
and rain—

birds diving
mice hiding

grasshoppers singing
spiders weaving—

in a sea of wheat
that will someday

become bread
we eat.

      —Irene Latham

*Green Wheat Fields,
Auvers* by Vincent
Van Gogh

WORDS FROM THE POET

Writing poems after artworks is a way to deepen our experiences with art. Our poems can ask—and answer—questions about the world. I especially enjoy discovering the unseen things hidden inside the piece, or just outside the frame. Poetry after art allows us to bring ourselves into the piece, not just as observers, but as participants.

CONSIDER THE TECHNIQUE

Ekphrasis means "description" in Greek, and in ancient times, ekphrastic poetry described anything from a fine article of clothing to a well-constructed building to a battle weapon. As humans, we naturally admire—describing, commenting, imagining—something made by hand. Today, ekphrastic poetry is written in response to art, but inspiration through artwork is not reserved for poets.

If you have visited an art museum, you have seen artists sitting and sketching, responding in ways that bring their own skills closer to those of the masters. Writers, always on the lookout for inspiration, also turn to art for ideas. Because every drawing, every clay pot, every bit of needlework grew from the mind and heart and hands and time period of another. From such handiwork, writers can grow their own written-word artwork—essay or novel, poem or argument. Vermeer painted his *Girl with a Pearl Earring* between 1665 and 1667, and Tracy Chevalier wrote her novel of the same title more than 330 years later. In this way, time seems to lose its bounds, and this mystery girl lives on beyond her death.

"Poetry after art allows us to bring ourselves into the piece, not just as observers, but as participants." Irene Latham's words encourage us to widen our worlds through art by bringing pen to page, lingering over an image long enough to uncover our own questions and beliefs, hopes and stories, fears and loves.

TRY IT

To find inspiring art, you might visit one of many online galleries or you might collect art postcards. Of course, you could also take a grand field trip—writing at the art museum! You might read books of poems inspired by art or visit Irene Latham's site, where she shares one ekphrastic poem each April day as part of her ArtSpeak! project.

Begin by looking at a piece of art. Talk together, listing and describing what you see. Then take a page from Latham's book and stroll "just outside the frame." What is happening before or after? What is hidden? Welcome students to pretend they see tiny things in the picture (as Latham "saw" mice and spiders) and imagine histories and words about the people and objects they see. You might model writing a free verse poem or notebook entry, weaving description and musing as you go.

Consider collaborating with another class or with your art teacher, swapping pieces of artwork and allowing these to inspire poetry or other forms of writing, as Amy Souza does with adults at Spark (getsparked.org). This makes for a lovely gallery showing, and sharing words and pictures between the youngest and oldest students is magical.

Most importantly, leave your students with the suggestion, "If ever you feel stuck for an idea, look at art. Let it lift you into new thoughts of your own."

A Few Places to Find Art for Writing Inspiration

- your school's art teacher—art teachers often have art posters and books to share

- postcards from a museum—you might keep a shoebox of these

- images from the National Gallery of Art online

- images from the Metropolitan Museum of Art online

A Few Poetry Collections Inspired by Art

- *Heart to Heart: New Poems Inspired by Twentieth-Century American Art* and *Side by Side: New Poems Inspired by Art from Around the World* by Jan Greenberg

- *Self-Portrait with Seven Fingers: The Life of Marc Chagall in Verse* by J. Patrick Lewis and Jane Yolen

- Irene Latham's "ArtSpeak!" page at her *Live Your Poem* blog

Hands Off the Paper

The hands are drawing by themselves
their hand are off the paper
All day all night they never cease
and will not stop forever
drawing the cuffs on their friends jacket
their hands are off the paper
always working never moving the shading gets no darker
these tired hands have never stopped
and will not stop forever
if you find them now you will see
their hands are off the paper

by-Luke C.
Grade 7

Poem inspired by

Drawing Hands
by M. C. Escher

Poem inspired by

The Starry Night
by Vincent van Gogh

Starry Starry Night

Cotch the breeze
and let it go

Wavy Curly clouds
the circle
the cold stars

The flowers
soak up
brightness but
not darkness

Climb up to the
tallest mountain
but still below
the sky

Relax in the
moon's bright
light

Starry starry Night

By: Jacob, 3rd grade

Just One Moon

Just one moon? Not ten? Not twenty?
You have to wonder: Why so few?
Even Mars, our nearest neighbor
(and inferior), has two.

Jupiter has sixty-seven—
Io, Carpo, Ganymede
(its moons need names to keep them straight,
confusion all but guaranteed).

Fourteen for Neptune. And for Saturn?
Sixty-two! Of all the things!
Unnecessarily messy and
excessive when you add the rings.

Still. Pluto doesn't even count
and it has five. We've been short-changed.
I'd like to see a coterie,
supposing that could be arranged.

Picture this: A twilight riot
as the sky fills up with moons
that polkadot the east horizon,
rising up like gold balloons.

Imagine, then, the multitude!
A horde, a herd, a throng, a tribe!
A merry mob of moonman faces
looming in the nighttime sky.

The dazzle of the full effect,
the gibbous troop, the crescent fleet,
the gleam of lunar luminescence
spilling onto city streets

would be a shimmerfest each evening
and bedazzling to behold,
but soon, like like phenomena,
would become commonplace and old.

Our moon commands our full attention,
tugging tides and marking time,
changing daily through the seasons,
arcing nightly through the sky.

Our single moon inspires reflection,
kindling myths to save and share
with all the people on our planet,
every culture, everywhere.

Just one moon. Not ten. Not twenty.
Just one moon, but one is plenty.

—*Susan Blackaby*

WORDS FROM THE POET

Posing a question helps get me started by catapulting an idea onto the blank page. My dad worked at NASA during the Apollo moon landings, and I know our moon has unique properties and influence that other planets' moons don't share—singular in every sense. Still. I wonder what it would be like to see a strand of moons, glowing like pearls in the night sky? Excellent question.

CONSIDER THE TECHNIQUE

If you have read Georgia Heard's *Awakening the Heart* (1999), you know about "the doors of poetry" (50–56). One of these is *wonder*. We can wonder about questions that seem small (Where are my glasses?) and questions that are clearly big (Why do people kill each other?). We can wonder about questions with answers (How do seeds travel?) and questions without answers (What is God?). Wonder sends our thinking down exquisitely surprising paths.

Questioning teaches us about the world, and a willingness to question is a citizen's responsibility. People who question find injustice and may work to combat this injustice. People who question find holes in what is commonly accepted and make new discoveries. When we ask questions, we learn new truths and uncover falsehoods.

In her poem, Susan Blackaby begins by questioning why Earth has but one moon and not more as other planets do. In her first few stanzas, the thought of many moons is fabulous, but as the poem continues Blackaby changes her mind, concluding with "one is plenty." When we ask questions and write, we figure out what we think. In the words of Flannery O'Connor, "I write because I don't know what I think until I read what I say" (quoted in Murray 1990, 8).

In *How to Get Your Child to Love Reading* (2003), Esmé Raji Codell recommends having children post questions on bulletin boards, adding answers as (or if) they find them. Wrapping our arms around the unknown is a wise way to make clear to students that asking matters. So often, children are taught to seek answers, and many answers are simply Google-able. But what about the questions that leave Siri and Google silent?

Along with so many other informational texts, the pregnancy bible *What to Expect When You're Expecting* by Heidi Murkoff and Sharon Mazel remains in print because it anticipates and then answers every question a pregnant woman could imagine. Essayists ask questions of themselves and of the world. And when reporters want to know more about something, they conduct interviews. Writing is a way to find answers and explore wonders.

TRY IT

Start wondering by taking a question hike. Walk with notebooks and pencils, jotting questions. Questions may be scientific or personal, silly or political. This question hike can be an actual walk by foot, or you might hike through books, inviting students to list questions as they read. Students might perform experiments or watch animals or study weather outside the classroom window, keeping question logs.

Ask students to think about books that may have been inspired by questions. Perhaps Natalie Babbitt wrote *Tuck Everlasting* because she was curious about immortality. Maybe Jeannine Atkins wrote *Stone Mirrors* because she had questions about the life of sculptor Edmonia Lewis.

In a wide-awake life, questions pop up regularly, and a writer's notebook is a perfect place to keep them. When a student asks an off-topic question or shares a curious thought, say, "Jot that question into your notebook—you might need it later." Have students keep a notebook page of questions, and when they choose writing topics for different genres, remind them to circle back to this page. Help young writers see that questions from months ago can inspire new ideas today.

STUDENT POEMS TO SHARE

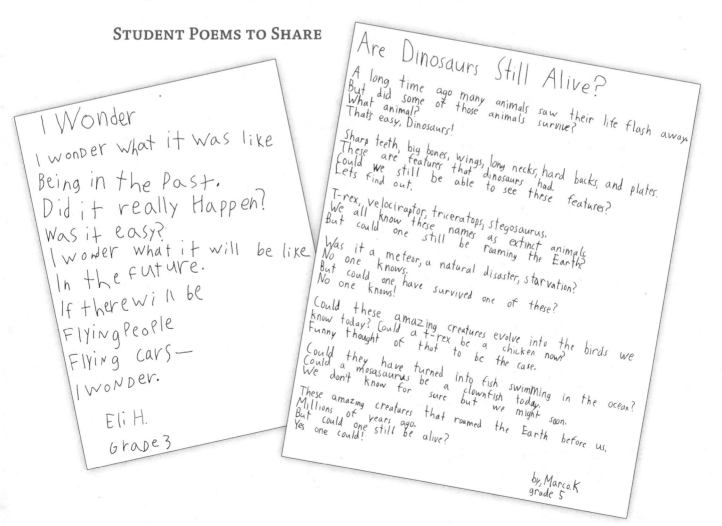

I Wonder

I wonder what it was like
Being in the Past.
Did it really Happen?
Was it easy?
I wonder what it will be like
In the future.
If there will be
Flying People
Flying cars—
I wonder.

Eli H.
Grade 3

Are Dinosaurs Still Alive?

A long time ago many animals saw their life flash away.
But did some of those animals survive?
What animal?
That's easy, Dinosaurs!

Sharp teeth, big bones, wings, long necks, hard backs, and plates.
These are features that dinosaurs had.
Could we still be able to see these features?
Lets find out.

T-rex, velociraptor, triceratops, stegosaurus.
We all know these names as extinct animals
But could one still be roaming the Earth?

Was it a meteor, a natural disaster, starvation?
No one knows.
But could one have survived one of these?
No one knows!

Could these amazing creatures evolve into the birds we know today? Could a t-rex be a chicken now?
Funny thought of that to be the case.

Could they have turned into fish swimming in the ocean?
Could a mosasaurus be a clownfish today?
We don't know for sure but we might soon.

These amazing creatures that roamed the Earth before us,
Millions of years ago.
But could one still be alive?
Yes one could!

by, Marco. K
grade 5

of c o u r s e:

t r u e   change is always   too   slow
and   o u r   b e s t   hopes rest with
s t e a d y
o n
beyond our own times

the   t r u e   revolutions   h a p p e n
within the covers of our best books
inside the noises of words with words
inside the movements of reading eyes

so:
the writers are   the   engines
the artists   are   the   engines
and the women   and   men
and the girls and   the   boys
reading   those   noisy books
all are   engines of true change

the words contain the power
and the books must have that
power and the noise of that
story and the shout of that song
must always be louder than the
silence of the bullets and the
silent deaths of grim despair

we m o v e forward with love

the s t r u g g l e c o n t i n u e s

—*arnold adoff*

© 2018 by Amy Ludwig VanDerwater, from *Poems Are Teachers*. Portsmouth, NH: Heinemann.

WORDS FROM THE POET

I began writing for kids because I wanted to effect a change in American society. I continue in that spirit. By the time we reach adulthood, we are closed and set in our attitudes. The chances of a poet reaching us are very slim. But I can open a child's imagination, develop his appetite for poetry, and more importantly, show him that poetry is a natural part of everyday life. We all need someone to point out that the emperor is wearing no clothes. That's the poet's job.

This poem has been with me for decades, . . . one of those strange continuations in a life of poetry. I shaped an early version for a poster my publisher created for my anthology The Poetry of Black America: Anthology of the 20th Century, *and I have shaped and changed and updated this piece several times, . . . most recently for a poster to celebrate the fortieth anniversary of the Coretta Scott King Book Awards.*

CONSIDER THE TECHNIQUE

Many texts grow from idea-and-belief-soil. Writers write about what they believe is important, what they believe is wrong, what they long to preserve. Editorial writers, reviewers, and cartoonists lay their beliefs bare on newsprint, greeting sleepy morning readers with coffee and opinion: Where is the hottest new restaurant in town? For whom should I vote? What's up with concussions in youth sports?

National Public Radio featured a show titled *This I Believe* for many years, and at the website thisibelieve.org you will find hundreds of belief essays by people of all ages and walks of life, essays about everything from attending funerals to being kind to the pizza dude.

In her book *Writing to Change the World* (2007), Mary Pipher asserts, "Writers can inspire a kinder, fairer, more beautiful world, or incite selfishness, stereotyping, and violence. Writers can unite people or divide them" (14). Arnold Adoff believes that as a poet, his job is to help people see that "the emperor is wearing no clothes." When we read his poem "of course:" we feel the power of books and artists and we feel the continued struggle. When we write, we nudge change, and it is our responsibility to think about what kind of writing change agents we wish to be. Which beliefs do we hold dear enough to share?

TRY IT

Your students will feel comfortable writing about feelings and beliefs if your classroom is a safe place where you model being vulnerable. Wiping tears during a read-aloud and stopping to say, "Let's take out our notebooks. I need to write," shows how feelings overflow from hearts onto notebook pages.

To help students think about their beliefs and feelings, read poems and books like Adoff's, asking, "What do you think this poet feels? What do his words make you believe?" Stop to write during a read-aloud or in the midst of a heated discussion. Read a quote or listen to a piece of music or share a statistic, and then write together: poetry, notebook entries, stories.

Or invite students to list feelings—happy, sad, fearful, embarrassed, furious, excited—and write from them. What beliefs do these feelings inspire? My feeling of peace while camping, for example, makes me believe that camping is mentally, spiritually, and physically healthy. I could write about that.

Offer questions that get at beliefs and feelings:

- What does this (story, quote, piece of art, song) lead you to feel? Believe?

- How are you different after reading/seeing this?

- What do you want to change in the world?

- For what are you grateful? Why?

- What do you believe is worth celebrating? Why?

- When do you feel most like you?

Regularly remind students that writing inspired by feelings and beliefs can nourish and impact readers—and our world.

A Few Poetry Collections Inspired by Feelings and Beliefs

- *Lend a Hand: Poems About Giving* by John Frank

- *Can I Touch Your Hair? Poems of Race, Mistakes, and Friendship* by Irene Latham and Charles Waters

- *Voice from Afar: Poems of Peace* by Tony Johnston

- *What the Heart Knows: Chants, Charms, and Blessings* by Joyce Sidman

I AM NOT GOING TO STOP WRITING

This is what I write
and I am not going to stop
I am who I am
so you can not change me
only I can change myself
and I know anyone can do the same
because we protect what we write
writing is fighting
By: Alvaro P.
3rd grade
morris Plains Borough school

Animals

The shining sun
in their eyes
They're lying high
They're lying low
The animals
roaming
Safe and sound
Until we had this idea
To take them out
The fur striped coats
And the
Shark fin soup
All this world needs is By: Ella B.
a little more peace Grade 4

The Longest Home Run

Mickey Mantle
New York Yankees
643 feet
September 10, 1960
Briggs Stadium, Detroit

was longer than
the Wright brothers flew in 15 seconds,
two Statues of Liberty,
three Goodyear blimps,
the width of four football fields,
five Douglas firs,
six blue whales,
seven Diplodocuses
or nine Great Sphinxes!

Your pick.

The Mick

—J. Patrick Lewis

WORDS FROM THE POET

For me, the strongest, most satisfying poems are rife with detail, *as is evident in "The Longest Home Run." I am impelled to write biographical poems, not only because there is, in my opinion, a dearth of them, but because you can pack so many circumstances of a moment, an event, a life in a few short lines.*

CONSIDER THE TECHNIQUE

I regularly consider the fact that I am a person living in the modern age, typing on my laptop, watering the peonies, feeding our dogs. So easily could I have been someone else, of a different gender and living in a different time. It is easy to become stuck here, understanding the world from my point of view, writing from only my experiences, seeing things in this one way, from this one small place in this one point in time.

Reading history allows us to briefly experience life as a different person—living, struggling, hoping—in another place and time. When we write from history, we are archaeologists holding words instead of pickaxes, peeling back layers of time to reveal story-fact-artifacts that we believe still matter. As J. Patrick Lewis says, "You can pack so many circumstances of a moment, an event, a life in a few short lines."

When reading the past, writers allow themselves to be moved. We might feel amazement, as Lewis is wowed by Mantle's record home run, or we might be enchanted by biography. When we learn about people who have beaten odds, shown kindness or cruelty, invented gadgets useful or not—we want to tell. And we do. We talk at the dinner table and hit "Share" on Facebook. But we can also make something new from days gone by. Just as my friend Eileen turns children's T-shirts into graduation quilts, the stories of long ago wait to be reshaped into articles, opinion pieces, and poetry.

I once read that a person dies two times, once when her body dies, and a second time when her name is spoken for the last time. So, occasionally, I walk through a cemetery, running my fingers over names carved in marble, saying names aloud. By doing so, I like to believe, I keep these names and people alive for another day. Similarly, we keep history alive when we write it. For as long as writers—in any genre—call up the people and places of long ago, they will not die. Gettysburg. Machu Picchu. Harriet Tubman.

TRY IT

First, read a bit of historical writing or look at a historical photo or video, related either to your current social studies unit or to a completely different time period. Ask students to talk about any of the following:

- How is this scene like our lives today? How is it different?

- If you could bring someone from this time period to life, what would you ask?

- What does this (photograph, story, set of facts) make you believe or help you know?

- What strikes you?

- Who interests you here?

After talking, write—go beyond facts, stretch into specific details, illuminate meaning. Notes like these might transform into informational articles, essays, or poems exploring history. Show students that writing from history is something they can do at any time, in any genre.

A Few Websites to Inspire History Writing

- National Archives

- Smithsonian

- Best of History Websites

A Few Poetry Collections Inspired by Historical Events

- *Rutherford B. Who Was He? Poems About Our Presidents* by Marilyn Singer

- *Good Masters! Sweet Ladies! Voices from a Medieval Village* by Laura Amy Schlitz

- *We Are America: A Tribute from the Heart* by Walter Dean Myers

Something Different

(a womans life in the 1800s)

Couldn't do certain things
Couldn't make your own
choices
Couldn't even get
a decent job

Every single day
Cook
Serve
clean
sew and wash

What if you refused
What if you did something
Different
Something you always dreamed of...

What if you were
One of those girls
Who made history
A girl
Who changed the world

By: clodagh B.
Grade 4

Why I cry...

I cry.
Why?
Because I got pushed out of my
home.
Why?
Because the Americans were...
What?
Greedy!
Why?
Because they wanted loads of land.
Why?
Because they wanted everything
Why?
They wanted to take over...
What?
Everything.
Why?
I don't know they're just...
What? what?
Greedy
Very Greedy!

By: Kari N.

Grade 4

Flood:
Ellicott City, Maryland

The river left its bed tonight,
woken by heavy rain.
It stomped down Main Street,
passed shops, houses
in a swirling rage. It's resting now.
We stare at empty spaces.

It whisked cars downhill.
Their underwater headlights
made an eerie glow. A chain
of strangers clasped arms,
pulled a woman from her spinning car.
A hillside washed away,
its green grass torn by claws
we did not know the river had.

It's resting now. We stare at empty spaces
where the river grabbed doors from hinges,
peeled away sidewalks, made off
with random things—bricks and jewels,
and two people—for no reason
other than they were in its path.

The river is resting. Now we stare
at empty spaces.

—*Laura Shovan*

© 2018 by Amy Ludwig VanDerwater, from *Poems Are Teachers*. Portsmouth, NH: Heinemann.

WORDS FROM THE POET

My town made national headlines when a flash flood tore apart our historic Main Street. Describing what I saw on the television news helped me reflect on the frightening images of this event. I think this is one reason why people write down their experiences during difficult times. For me, a poem is a safe place to write about emotions like shock and grief. Whether you record a true event in a poem, essay, journal, or work of fiction, writing is also a way to share those feelings with others.

CONSIDER THE TECHNIQUE

In the same way the ocean tosses new shells and bits of glass on the sand, the world throws hundreds of new topics at us each day. Picture-book writers and novelists alike find topics in news and inspiration in current events. For example, both Eve Bunting's picture book *Ducky* and Donovan Hohn's adult nonfiction book *Moby-Duck* recount the real journey of rubber animals gone overboard in the Pacific Ocean in 1992.

Current news stories might make us angry or sad or joyful, and writing gives us a way to give our feelings and reactions form. We listen to today's news, and then tomorrow we open the newspaper (or screen) to find out what writers think about it. Opinion columnists such as Leonard Pitts and Gail Collins and George Will read about events and think, "I must speak up." Our students can too. Regardless of beliefs, writers transform what they read in daily headlines into other genres: story, opinion, poetry.

In "Flood," we sense Laura Shovan's fear and surprise at the power of water. By writing about a news story close to home, she is able to work through her response to the event and also bring it to a larger audience.

TRY IT

Make news sharing a regular part of your day and encourage students to share articles that bring up questions or new ideas. You can contribute too, sharing articles you feel match your students' interests and concerns. Give students time to write "off of" news articles or brief current video clips, challenging them to capture their thinking, connections, concerns, and hopes. They can draft notebook entries or even free verse poems that may stay poems—or may inspire longer essays, fiction, or nonfiction writing.

You might make a nested circle diagram—me/hometown/country/ world—placing circle within circle, listing events in various places and discussing how they affect you. Or you might ask students to list in their notebooks news stories they remember, perhaps under various categories—nature news, town news, big world news—and then to choose one and write about it. For a sense of perspective, invite older adults to your class and ask them to share news events that changed them.

When students write in any genre, offer writing-from-news as a possible idea collecting strategy. From these entries, young writers can experiment with writing about the same topic from various points of view. Or you might ask, "What does this event bring to mind? What will you write from it?"

A Few Online News Sources for Classrooms

- NPR

- The New York Times Learning Network

- Newsela

- Scholastic News

STUDENT POEMS TO SHARE

What Ifs

As we wait in the field like crippled mice
for the Serbs—the hawks—to kill us,
a funny thought occurs to me.

What if when Edvin—my best friend—
fled with his family, my family had followed?

What if—eight days ago—when the Serbs came
to our home in Foca to deliver a first—and final—warning
to leave or be murdered—our family had left?

What if Father had not instead
grabbed the gun of the first,
shot the second
and gotten shot by the third,
all while yelling at us to run?

What if I had grabbed Mother, as well as Mirsada,
as I heeded his advice?

What if I had not run at all?

Perhaps carpets would still hang on the walls
and lie on the floor
like familiar and beautiful creatures
reminding us
that everything was how it should be.
Perhaps I would be sipping my morning kava
instead of letting the last few raindrops
fall on my tongue.

As the Serbs turn away, toward the west,
I turn toward the east.
Toward Croatia.
Toward hope.

I take Mirsada's hand
and we walk
into the sunrise.

By Alex C.
Grade 8

Thursday Happenings

Great things happen on Thursdays
Spicy chicken and black rice happen.
Friendship happens
Love happens
Birthdays and graduations happen

There are voices that sound like 1920's jazz
Poets who write like Langston Hughes
Girls who are friends to everyone
Men who love engine repair

Out of anger and death come flowers
In a year of despair and vulgarity, talents shine through
Out of drugs and abuse come college educations
Out of AOK comes life

by George S.
grade 7

Inspired by "The Power of a Dinner Table"
by David Brooks (2016)

A Rumble in My Bedroom

There's a rumble in my bedroom
that I've never felt before.
I can see it on the ceiling.
I can feel it in the floor.

All my furniture is juddering
and jumping 'round the room,
and the sound is loud and pounding
like a constant sonic boom.

There's a banging and a clanging
and a thudding and a thumping.
I can barely even stand
with all the shaking and the bumping.

It began this way just yesterday.
It hasn't let up yet,
since I found a bounding elephant
and kept him as a pet.

—*Kenn Nesbitt*

WORDS FROM THE POET

After spending a few weeks pondering what-if ideas (*"what if I were the president,"* *"what if aliens invaded," and so on), I landed on "what if I had a pet elephant." To make it more interesting, though, I decided to describe what might happen, but save the explanation for a small surprise at the end.*

My favorite poems are ones that bring a smile to the reader's face. Often, I create funny poems by combining ideas that don't normally go together, such as ballet-dancing pirates, piano-playing pets, or astronaut cows. I'll ask myself what might happen if such a thing occurred, and then begin to write. The resulting poem is usually completely absurd, which is just the way I like it.

CONSIDER THE TECHNIQUE

When taking to the page, writers consider what-is, what-is-not, what-could-be, and what-could-never-be. At times the what-could-be is serious: "What if we do not take steps to protect our environment?" At times it is playful: "What if a spoiled and lonely girl learned of a secret garden?" We humans can imagine all kinds of *what if*s: funny, serious, sad, joyous.

Many of our students' favorite books mix reality and imagination. Authors such as Roald Dahl take the real world (chocolate factories exist) and add a pinch of *what if* (What if a chocolate factory could make all kinds of fantastic chocolates and candies?). When Dahl was a boy, students at his boarding school were regularly sent new Cadbury chocolates to review. As an adult, Dahl remembered his childhood dreams of inventing new candies. Ta-da! *Charlie and the Chocolate Factory*. (Read more about Roald Dahl's writing-from-*what-if* at his website.)

Whether it's predicting the fallout from world events or warning parents of the possible consequences of parenting mistakes, opinion writers and commentators often rely on a *what if* stance. *What if* gets us thinking.

In the poem "A Rumble in My Bedroom," Kenn Nesbitt's speaker appears to be a regular person with what at first might seem a regular problem. His bedroom is a recognizable bedroom (we are in our own world), and the noise and shaking is exceptional (could it be an earthquake?) but not outlandish. Only at the end do we sense the whimsy in the joy of an elephant-surprise. We take delight in his *what if* as it takes us beyond what we expect and bumps against all we know about having pets.

The question of *what if* is one that our youngest children know well. Dress-up is a form of *what if*, as is playing in a blanket fort. For a child, anything is possible. For a child, the world is full of *what if*. As writers, we work to come back to that place.

TRY IT

One way to brainstorm writing ideas from *what if* is simply to daydream for a few moments. I sometimes lie on my couch, letting go of to-do lists and worries, opening my mind for new possibilities. And while you cannot provide couches for all your students, you can teach them to close their eyes and to wait and listen for ideas. Model by closing your eyes and saying, "I am going to close my eyes and imagine a *what if* or two. What if a mouse ran across the floor in class? What if everyone could read each other's thoughts for just one hour?" Invite students to do the same and then write silently from whatever this imagining yields. Or have students make T-charts, listing real things from their lives on one side, and inventing corresponding *what if*s on the other.

Invite students to ask *what if?* when they write in different genres. What if we could fly without airplanes? What if a boy could be a girl for a day? What if people of opposing political parties listened carefully to each other? Students who have not had much experience daydreaming may at first struggle to go beyond the stories they have watched on screens or played in video games. Or they may go hog-wild, their *if*s so far-fetched that they are difficult for readers to understand. This is to be expected, but with time and practice, the muscle of the imagination will become strong. Be patient.

STUDENT POEMS TO SHARE

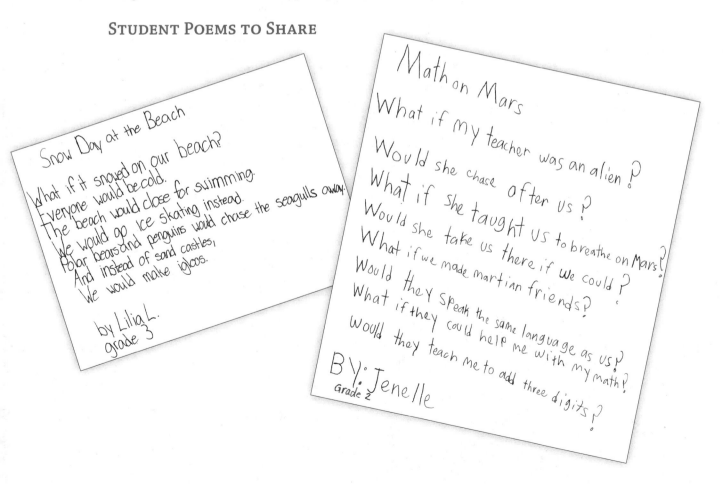

Snow Day at the Beach

What if it snowed on our beach?
Everyone would be cold.
The beach would close for swimming.
We would go ice skating instead.
Polar bears and penguins would chase the seagulls away.
And instead of sand castles,
We would make igloos.

by Lilia L.
grade 3

Math on Mars

What if my teacher was an alien?
Would she chase after us?
What if she taught us to breathe on Mars?
Would she take us there if we could?
What if we made martian friends?
Would they speak the same language as us?
What if they could help me with my math?
Would they teach me to add three digits?

BY: Jenelle
Grade 2

Old Barn

The old barn at the edge of our yard
Housed horses once,
Long before I was born.

The pale barn with a sunken roof,
Draped with icicle and snow,
Shone red as a windfall apple.

The cold barn, black holes in its slats,
With a hayloft and a high swinging door,
Stood through every winter storm.

The old barn at the edge of our yard
Housed horses once,
Weathered, warped, and worn.

—*Steven Withrow*

© 2018 by Amy Ludwig VanDerwater, from *Poems Are Teachers*, Portsmouth, NH: Heinemann.

WORDS FROM THE POET

A poem describing an object is more like a painting than a photograph—it's a blend of observation and imagination. My poem combines simple details of sight and touch to create the barn's image in the reader's mind, and I moved outside the present moment to give the barn a vivid history. When writing, you're free to choose how you project what your senses tell you.

For this poem, I stood at various distances from the barn so that I could see it as a part of its environment (far away), as an object in itself (middle distance), and as a collection of tiny details (up close). I drew on all three to write the poem. It's that scientific idea of a parallax, where the farther away you are from something, the smaller it appears to you, and vice versa. It's important to seek out different distances and angles from something, even imagining the object from the inside out.

CONSIDER THE TECHNIQUE

Not long ago, as I shopped in a local store, the clerk half-answered my questions as he half-played a video game. His phone rested near the register, and I watched as this young man's finger swiped to shoot or score as he took occasional glances up at me. The ability to juggle many things (and people) at once might be considered productive, but this disjointed attention is the opposite of what a writer needs to create scenes and images readers that can inhabit.

Writing requires focused attention, and young writers must learn how to observe and describe—to show and not tell, as they say. We all absorb information through our senses, but many ignore this information while writing, describing objects in general terms as a child might draw a generic house with a square bottom and a triangle top. Steven Withrow reminds us that we are free to choose how we share the information from our senses, and also to blend observation and imagination. We see how he does this, bringing an old barn to full color and life through close looking with careful words.

To become careful observers, students need opportunities to slow down and focus on their senses. In *The Listening Walk* by Paul Showers, a young girl decides to take her usual walk to the park while paying close attention to every sound. When we read this book, our own ears perk up as we experience new sounds in a new place. We can take walks, too. We, too, can practice paying attention to one sense at a time.

Writers of every genre rely on observation to strengthen their texts. By looking deeply and describing carefully, writers welcome readers to try a dissection at the lab, watch the kitten sleeping in a square of sun, or rummage through Great-Grandmother's quilt drawer. Writers are awake to buildings and animals, textures and sounds, all around—watching, sketching, and writing these alive for readers.

TRY IT

You may not be able to slow all of time down, but you can slow a bit of time, cupping your hands around it as you might protect a small flame. And when you do this, you demonstrate how to deeply look, touch, feel, listen, taste.

Choose something to observe together. It might be a class fern or a small corner of a familiar courtyard. It might be a patch of autumn sky with clouds a-racing. It might be your own fingerprint or a friend's iris or a single leaf. Now, sense by sense, ask students to list what they observe. Make comparisons. Use color words. Try new adjectives. Choose simple nouns (leaf, clothes, dessert), and then make these more specific (aspen leaf, woolen sock, blackberry pie). Once everyone has a few observation lists, invite your young writers to grow a notebook entry from a list or two.

> The Private Eye (5X) Looking/Thinking by Analogy is a wonderful curriculum focused on observation and connections between art, science, and writing. Check out the books, workshops, and online resources.

Discuss how looking closely can offer writing ideas. What does this pile of snow make you think about? What story might you imagine from the watch on your arm, from this scuffed floor or that bright tulip? Through close observation, students come to understand big ideas ("Old barns should be preserved"), discover hidden stories ("Once a lost kitten found shelter in a barn"), and find subjects they wish to learn more about ("What is it like to be a dairy farmer?"). Observing offers ideas.

Draw as observation practice. When I taught fifth grade, I placed thirty acorns in the middle of the room. Each student selected one and drew it respectfully, knowing we would soon return them to the pile. Once we returned them, each of us used our drawings to find our own acorns. Since most acorns look quite similar, we really had to study those little guys, had to notice each ridge, each small hole, each curve. We needed to observe.

A Few Poetry Books Inspired by Close Observation

- *All the Small Poems and Fourteen More* by Valerie Worth
- *Fresh Delicious: Poems from the Farmers' Market* by Irene Latham
- *Hummingbird Nest: A Journal of Poems* by Kristine O'Connell George

Apple

My Apple is like an earth,
Spinning around in the atmosphere.
It has layers, like we live on the Skin of Earth
With dots like Stars in the SKY.
Green and smooth.

by Jaubert B.
grade 4

Goodbye Winter

Winter has just sixweeks left,
Now that groundhog saw his shadow.
But it seems like spring,
Since the last sign of the cold season
Is the bright red berry tree.
Dozens of bright red,
Inedible fruit,
Sprawl up from the small tree's root.
Only burst of color,
Against some almost melted snow.
Well,
More winter wouldn't hurt.

By Miriam T.
Grade 3

Night

Stars wink, dodging
in and out of darkness.

Much science starts with seeing
but questions push past surfaces.
How big and blustery are stars?
How old is their dust and light?
How far away do they shine?

Answers change into new questions
the way wonder turns to words
then back again to wonder.

Look up at the night sky.

—*Jeannine Atkins*

WORDS FROM THE POET

Both poets and scientists may look closely at the world, make mistakes, try again, and wonder. I write starting with what I see, then ask what science can and can't say about its power and patterns. What can one specific moment tell me about the universe?

CONSIDER THE TECHNIQUE

As I write these words, my husband enters our messy dining room, headlamp in hand, issuing an invitation, "Supreme nature moment! Outside near the basement doors, a mother wolf spider's abdomen is covered with babies. This spider will make all other spiders in your life seem small."

I follow Mark outside to look at this enormous mom, remembering back to when I carried one baby on my own back, pushed another in a stroller, and held one by her small hand. For a moment, I am this spider, and she is me. My mind fills with questions. Exactly how many babies are riding upon her back? Do all spiders do this? How long will the little ones stay there? Does she feed them? Do spider babies ever fall off of their moms? What then? And what about my own babies, now almost grown themselves?

From sitting at our kitchen table to estimating the number of spiderlings on a mama's back, my mind quickly shifts. Could I write a poem about this? An essay about how all moms are alike in certain ways? Could I write a picture book about spiders? I am reminded of Nicola Davies' picture book *I Don't Like Snakes*, with its text switching between the story of a girl who does not like snakes and the fascinating-fact-snake-information touted by her family members. Perhaps I could try something like this myself.

"Questions push past surfaces," Jeannine Atkins writes. As a writer married to a science teacher, I understand daily the closeness of writing and science. When we encourage our students to experiment with floating paper clips and sinking shells, we ask them to play and discover. Writers play and discover too.

Our whole physical world is governed by the laws of science, and to be truly alive is to be curious about how it all works. If you have ever listened to National Public Radio's *Radiolab* podcast, you have been drawn into stories of helpful parasites, morality, the periodic table, and ancient lobsters. "Whoa, that's pretty neat," you might think. "Yuck," you might think. But whether intrigued or grossed out, writers and scientists alike act as Chiefs of Curiosity.

"Hey, look!" we can say, slowing down as we head to the playground. "Do you see that bird? It's called a cardinal, and the males are much brighter than the females." Like my husband, we can invite our students to watch for tonight's glory of a full moon and talk the next day about what they noticed. As Atkins asks, so do we, "What can one specific moment tell me about the universe?"

TRY IT

Finding ideas in science is an option when we build rituals around reading and talking about science. A comment as simple as, "I read this amazing article about wolf spiders last night, and I might write about it today," models how to find writing ideas in science. Subscribe as a class to a science magazine such as *Ask* or *Muse*, or read science articles at Wonderopolis.org so students see science as a writing-idea treasure chest.

Make time for reflective writing during science, or bring experiments into writing workshops and introduce scientific observation. As Jeannine Atkins writes, "I write starting with what I see." Offer students interesting things to see—snake skins, pulleys, baking soda and vinegar rockets—and encourage them to write poems and thoughts and ideas.

Writing outdoors is another way to pique interest in science and spur writing. In *Last Child in the Woods: Saving Our Children from Nature-Deficit Disorder* (2005), author Richard Louv writes, "Everything is phenomenal; everything is incredible; never treat life casually" (292).

By regularly writing and talking about science, you will lift your students' curiosity building interest in subjects they may choose to pursue as writers . . . or even as professionals one day.

A Few Poetry Books Inspired by Science

- *The Tree That Time Built: A Celebration of Nature, Science, and Imagination* by Mary Ann Hoberman and Linda Winston

- *Winter Bees and Other Poems of the Cold; Dark Emperor and Other Poems of the Night;* and *Song of the Water Boatman and Other Pond Poems* by Joyce Sidman

- *Random Body Parts: Gross Anatomy Riddles in Verse* by Leslie Bulion

- *The Poetry of Science: The Poetry Friday Anthology for Science* by Sylvia Vardell and Janet Wong

The New Brother

Earth our planet,
Earth our home,
Is there another like you?

Earth our planet,
Earth our home,
We have found your long lost brother.

Kepler-254b is his name.
He has your water.
He has your land.

He may be bigger,
He may be farther away.
He may contain other life.

But Earth our planet,
Earth our home,
Will you still be ours?

Earth our planet,
Earth our home,
We may leave you for your brother.

by Kayli V.
grade 8

R is for Redwood

I am the great Hyperion,
the tallest Redwood found.
15 feet in diameter.
379 feet from the ground.
And though I am so very tall,
I dont get taller very fast
for but 1 inch per year I grow
Yet here I am, rising slowly,
loyal, strong, steadfast.

by Georgia V., grade 5

Things We Prize

Hidden in the mountains, fed by snow,
The lake was small. We stayed there every year
And got to know our neighbors camping near
In tents like toadstools growing in a row.

I found a secret pool, a little nook
Where I could lie and watch the fish below
But no amount of coaxing made them go
For worms, or bits of bacon on my hook.

At last a fish too hungry to be wise
Took my bait so hard its body shook.
"A fish!" I cried. "Big enough to cook!"
I held it high to show its mighty size.

Even though the lake is far away
I remember posing with my prize
And grinning at our neighbors' happy cries
Just as though it happened yesterday.

I've caught some bigger fish but this is clear,
They'll never match the thrill I felt that day.
No matter what those larger trophies weigh
The first fish will always be most dear.

—*David L. Harrison*

© 2018 by Amy Ludwig VanDerwater, from *Poems Are Teachers*. Portsmouth, NH: Heinemann.

WORDS FROM THE POET

Our memories take us back to times that helped shape us. Thinking about this favorite memory was like looking at pictures in a scrapbook. In my mind I still don my Davy Crockett coonskin cap and explore the piney woods of Whitehorse Lake in northern Arizona. I still grip a baseball, with the seams just so. Wince at a snakebite. Write my sweetheart's name again and again. Play my trombone as couples sway. I am husband who pulled flowers I thought were weeds. Father who paid my kids a nickel for every bagworm picked. I am scientist. Editor. Businessman. Writer. My experiences are the stitches that bind me together.

CONSIDER THE TECHNIQUE

As writers, we carry our memories with us always, and each one holds possibilities for writing in all genres. Our opinions, passions, loves, and fears germinate in our individual histories. In *The Things They Carried*, Vietnam War veteran and National Book Award winner Tim O'Brien blends his memories serving in Vietnam with fiction. Patricia Polacco, author and illustrator of many memoirs, introduces readers to a treasured family quilt in *The Keeping Quilt*, the meteor from her grandparents' yard in *Meteor!*, and her teacher in *Thank You, Mr. Falker*. The idea for my own nonfiction picture book, *Every Day Birds*, grew from memories of my husband teaching our family the names of birds. These memories made me wish to pass this information-gift on to children.

"My experiences are the stitches that bind me together," writes David L. Harrison. At any time, we can invite students to examine their own stitches for writing possibilities—places they have been, people they have known, songs they have sung, dishes they have tasted, books they have read, every smooth stone they have ever rubbed between their fingers, every fear they have ever felt. When we read Harrison's words to our students, we can ask, "What do you still do in your own mind, the way David Harrison still plays trombone and yanks flowers instead of weeds?" And when they answer, we can smile and offer time to write.

TRY IT

Make memory mining a regular part of writing time by offering your students brief exercises that help them explore their own pasts. You can do this throughout the year, not only during units of narrative. After all, our opinions sprout from our memories, as do our information-interests. A student who remembers talking with her uncle about his time as a soldier may choose to research PTSD, writing an informational article, or from this same memory she may write an essay about how war affects the human spirit.

Sketching, listing, and writing about memory can awaken forgotten thoughts. Ask your students to close their eyes and think silently about any one of the ideas on this list, or any other memory-invoking idea, and then write.

- favorite toys

- foods with stories

- times you learned something new

- holiday traditions

- words your (grandma, father, mother, sister, brother) always says

- changes

- songs that make you remember

- smells that call up people and places

Students can keep memory pages in their notebooks and revisit these pages when writing in different genres, expanding their thoughts and thinking toward audience. For an essay they might ask, "What do I believe now because of this memory?" or for informational writing, "What does this memory make me want to learn or teach?"

A Few Poetry Books Inspired by Memories

- *Baseball, Snakes, and Summer Squash: Poems About Growing Up* by Donald Graves

- *A Fire in My Hands* by Gary Soto

- *Stepping Out with Grandma Mac* by Nikki Grimes

- *Been to Yesterdays: Poems of a Life* by Lee Bennett Hopkins

Turtles

Rolo melts
in a pretzel
and under a pecan
during christmas time.
We give it to
my Grandpa

I watch him
open it.
I play in the
basement after presents.

As we go
I look at
the box —
They are gone!

by Walter Z.
grade 3.

Wesley

Sunny
Warm
Playing teaball
Wesley's gramparants waching

Curly blond hair
Wesley hit ball
me next
hit ball
Flew over the fence over
over
and over

again daddy runs to get it
over
over
and over again.

Natalie F.
Grade 3

Star Stuff

A boy once told me,
We are made of star stuff.
I imagined bits of shine
broken off from stars inside us.
He meant, we are made of divine ingredients—
calcium in our teeth, iron in our blood,
every atom in our bodies crafted
in the kiln of long-dead stars.
You. Me.
Those we've never met,
might never know,
in cities and towns we've only read the names of—
kids playing soccer barefoot in the streets of Rio,
a girl riding her bike to school in Accra,
even the boy in Orion, Alabama
gazing up at the spattered canvas of night—
all of us plaited together by stars.
On starry nights
mothers, fathers, friends
we've lost
wink at us.

We are made of stars,
we dazzle.

—*Georgia Heard*

© 2018 by Amy Ludwig VanDerwater, from *Poems Are Teachers*. Portsmouth, NH: Heinemann.

WORDS FROM THE POET

This poem, and many of my poems, start with a sense of awe. A heart flutter. Joy. My work in writing a poem is to be the conductor of a chorus: holding the aha *moment in my heart; painting images with words; and harmonizing with rhythm and sound.*

CONSIDER THE TECHNIQUE

Dictionary.com defines *awe* as "an overwhelming feeling of reverence, admiration, fear, etc., produced by that which is grand, sublime, extremely powerful, or the like: *in awe of God; in awe of great political figures.*" Awe guides many writers to pen, many painters to easel.

Our students have grown up hearing the word *awesome* tossed about like a football, and due to overuse, it does not feel as weighty as it means. To be awed, we must be openhearted enough to be moved by a scene, a person, a moment. To be awed, we must be able-to-be-impressed. In our YouTube world, some of our students will need us to model true awe, and we can do this by slowing down, breathing deeply, and publicly appreciating corners of our glorious world.

Describing herself as "the conductor of a chorus," Georgia Heard expresses what writers often wish to do, to transmit their own "*aha* moment" to others. If you've ever read a life-changing book, been brought to tears by a song, or stood at the edge of Niagara Falls, you know what it's like to stand, eyes wide, pointing to the rushing water. So it is with writing from awe. We have been changed—and we long to share.

Many authors write from this feeling of admiration and astonishment. David McCord, the first winner of the NCTE Excellence in Poetry for Children Award, reminds us, "One of my teachers told me, 'Never let a day go by without looking on three beautiful things.' I try to live up to that and find it isn't difficult. The sky in all weathers is, for me, the first of these three things. This is wise advice for any writer—or any liver—of any age" (quoted in Cullinan 1995, 3).

Upon first glance, this learning-to-be-amazed might not feel like a writing lesson, but it is perhaps one of the most important lessons we can teach. Honor gorgeousness. Celebrate that which amazes you and speeds your heartbeat. Allow yourself to feel small. Place yourself in situations that remind you of the fleetingness of time, the magnificence of nature or of human accomplishment. Gasp. Then write.

TRY IT

I remember the third-grade teacher who told me, "Every year, on the day of the first snow, I always bring the children outside. We stand in a circle, hold hands, and I teach them to catch snowflakes on their tongues."

Modeling awe is not a computer lesson, not a lesson to be taught from a screen. Here is where you find three-dimensional, tangible-world opportunities to be wowed. And you allow your students to see you, mouth gaping, amazed. Tell them, "Sometimes the world will amaze you and make you feel small—in a good way. At those times, a writing idea is tapping on your shoulder saying, 'Write about me.'"

Discuss when students have stood in wonder, almost broken open by something powerful or lovely. It is important to model ways to take in this planet full of inspiration. The story you reverently tell about watching a sunrise with your dog will stay with your students. It will teach them that awe holds ideas.

Make space for awe in your classroom. Begin with natural beauties: dandelion, sparkly stone, pale blue sky. Like McCord and Heard, you can always look to the sky, perhaps even keeping a class weather journal or sky sketchbook. You might invite an inspiring elder to speak, one with many stories and much wisdom to share, or visit somewhere old together: a historic house, a cemetery, a massive tree. Place your students squarely in the middle of something awesome, and then give time to write.

If your school is situated in a neighborhood where children do not immediately see the natural wonders of stars and sea, meadow and mountain, teach them to find awe in different places. Read *Something Beautiful* by Sharon Dennis Wyeth or *Last Stop on Market Street* by Matt de la Peña. Be awed by people, by buildings, by wind. Pay attention to the shimmery feathers on a pigeon's neck or to that tiny snowman at the bus stop. Read Eve Bunting's *Anna's Table*, then replace a computer desk with a nature table and fill it with treasures. After all, as Heard reminds us, "We are made of stars." May we be dazzled as we dazzle.

Bird's song

The bird's song fly
through the canyon
through the stars
to the moon
and you wish
The song falls from the sky
to the canyon
To hear the bird's song...
something
besides silence

by Aiden P.   Grade 4

The World Is So Big

The world is so big.
There is lots to see and do.
More people to meet...
New friends to make...
things to learn...
and emotions to feel.
You won't always get along
with people you know and will know
But when in doubt
Just remember...
the world is so Big
By Emmett M.
Grade 5

Brand-New Roller Skate Blues
(for Bessie Smith)

She won a singing contest at the age of eight.
Won a silver dollar singing at the age of eight.
She saved her prize to buy some brand-new roller skates.

Baby, don't you know that gal could sing so fine.
Oh, baby don't you know that gal could sing so fine.
She sang her way to stardom at the age of nine.

The girl left Chattanooga with a minstrel show.
Rode out of Chattanooga with a minstrel show.
She wailed the blues from Georgia up to Ohio.

She strutted across the stage in gowns and satin shoes.
Chile, she strutted cross the stage in gowns and satin shoes.
No wonder they all called her the "Empress of the Blues."

—*Carole Boston Weatherford*

© 2018 by Amy Ludwig VanDerwater, from *Poems Are Teachers*. Portsmouth, NH: Heinemann.

WORDS FROM THE POET

As an author, I mine the past for family stories, fading traditions, and forgotten heroes. I am drawn to achievers and activists who overcame adversity and made history. I research my subjects through print, images, audio, and video. I also ask the ancestors to speak to and through me. They have never let me down.

CONSIDER THE TECHNIQUE

People love talking and reading about other people. Brandon Stanton's books *Humans of New York* and *Humans of New York: Stories,* as well as his blog, *Humans of New York,* are wildly popular as they share stories of New Yorkers of all ages and backgrounds interviewed by author/photographer/blogger Stanton. National Public Radio programs *This American Life* and *StoryCorps* celebrate people's lives, quirks, similarities, and differences. Readers are nosy.

Biographies are a popular nonfiction genre for young and old alike, and we find them in picture books and thick adult hardcovers. People read about inventors, politicians, athletes, musicians, actors, authors, military generals, artists, revolutionaries. I even like reading obituaries, considering the lives of others whose time has intersected with mine. Evidently I am not alone. William McDonald recently published *The New York Times Book of the Dead: 320 Print and 10,000 Digital Obituaries of Extraordinary People.*

Reading and writing about other people can help us understand ourselves. We may feel fortunate for what we have or strive for something new. We may see qualities in strangers we do not wish to emulate, and we may learn about people who show levels of kindness or dedication that challenge us. Writing about people also offers us a way to think about not only stories but opinions. What do we *believe* about what this person did? We can collect information and teach others about fascinating people who led interesting lives.

Many people create family trees, searching for names, connections, and clues about relatives. And many others make beautiful scrapbooks, collecting quotes and moments of their loved ones' lives. As Carole Boston Weatherford writes, "I mine the past for family stories, fading traditions, and forgotten heroes." In the lives of people, we find all of these.

TRY IT

Several categories of people might inspire writing:

- people you know: family, friends, neighbors

- strangers you encounter

- historical figures you admire, dislike, wish to learn about

- athletes, artists, singers
- people on the world or community stage right now
- ancestors you know or have never met
- people in photographs
- characters from books, movies, childhood stories
- names straight from the phone book or gravestones
- people you invent

Encourage students to keep lists of interesting people in their notebooks. Pause during science and history and math to think about the people behind the content. Who were they? Why did they do these things? Read poems and books inspired by people, books such as *Amazing Faces* by Lee Bennett Hopkins.

We are each members of various communities (family, neighborhood, town, school, church, synagogue, mosque, club, chorus, team), and you can help students see the potential in writing about people they work and play with each day. Second graders near my home wrote opinion pieces about local people, celebrating their greatness with written awards such as "Kindest Bus Driver" and "Most Helpful Neighbor." Winners were invited to an award celebration, complete with doughnuts from the PTO. One child read her poem to her brother, serving overseas, via Skype.

When students understand that people can serve as inspiration for writing, they never need another source. What to do today? Well, I can write about that little girl I just saw at T. J. Maxx, the way she held a brown oak leaf in her tiny hands, the way she twirled it around as her mom shopped for boots.

A Few Poetry Books Inspired by People

REAL PEOPLE

- *All by Herself* by Ann Whitford Paul
- *Bravo! Poems About Amazing Hispanics* by Margarita Engle
- *Heroes and She-roes: Poems of Amazing and Everyday Heroes* and *When Thunder Comes: Poems for Civil Rights Leaders* by J. Patrick Lewis

FICTIONAL PEOPLE

- *Bronzeville Boys and Girls* by Gwendolyn Brooks
- *Fathers, Mothers, Sisters, Brothers: A Collection of Family Poems* by Mary Ann Hoberman

- *The Last Fifth Grade of Emerson Elementary*
  by Laura Shovan
- *Hopscotch Love: A Family Treasury of Love Poems*
  by Nikki Grimes

STUDENT POEMS TO SHARE

Mom
You are gorgeous
With your flowers
in your hair

and you hair is brown
and you are blooming
flowers from your

hair
You're like summer!

by Noah S. grade 2

Christopher Columbus

Starting off as just a weaver
Four siblings, poor family.

Did you know
you'd become a famous sailor?

Discovering the Americas,
Supported by the monarchs of Spain?

Then becoming a notorious sailor
by getting slaves to search for gold.

Dishonored is what you became
by keeping it all for yourself.

Soon after dying with a horrifying disease
Your name living forever.

by Amanda W.
grade 5

Tree House

You are planks and nails, walls and floor
Nothing more, some say
I say no way

You are my tree house
My waiting for me house
My crow's nest over the Baltic Sea house

You are whatever I need you to be, house
My nobody knows where I am—I'm free house
My "Let's have a tea party, just you and me" house
My "OK, squeeze in, but just us three" house

You are my come in, no need for a key house
My rocket-fueled racecar to win the Grand Prix house
My prairie as far as my eyes can see house
My drowsy laze to the buzz of a bee house

You are planks and nails,
walls and floor,
but so much
more,
my house that is me
house

—*Laura Purdie Salas*

© 2018 by Amy Ludwig VanDerwater, from *Poems Are Teachers*. Portsmouth, NH: Heinemann.

WORDS FROM THE POET

When I write about a place, I'm usually not trying to just describe it physically. I'm trying to capture and share how that place makes me feel. My tree house was a place of possibilities and pretending, so I wrote a list poem that showed many different roles my tree house played, and I picked a meter, or rhythm, that swings easily from one line to the next to reflect that quick-change ability. I also listed positive and fun or peaceful activities. If I had called it a prison and a dungeon, that would have told the reader I felt an entirely different way about this place!

CONSIDER THE TECHNIQUE

Places inspire. When you read Laura Purdie Salas' poem "Tree House," you may have been reminded of a secret place from your own childhood. I remembered the forts my sister and I made in the rocky fields behind our home, forts made of rock borders, forts like the ones in Alice McLerran's *Roxaboxen*.

At five, before the days of rock forts, I sat under the lilac bushes bordering our yard and tore heart-shaped leaves into green snowflakes. At ten, I slept over at my great-aunt Kay's house, and I can still see the tiny (untouchable) rose-shaped soaps in her bathroom and the fancy couch in her living room. As a mom today, I strive to create a home full of pets and adventure, a place I hope our children will remember fondly. The places we have been help us know who we are and what we think is important. And places give us writing ideas.

Many favorite picture books are inspired by place. Patricia McLachlan's *All the Places to Love* and *What You Know First* remind us of where we begin. *Our Tree Named Steve* by Alan Zweibel and *Letting Swift River Go* by Jane Yolen celebrate child-loved places now gone.

The spectacular informational book *Atlas Obscura: An Explorer's Guide to the World's Hidden Wonders* (2016) by Joshua Foer, Dylan Thuras, and Ella Morton (and the website of the same name) takes readers on a journey to visit more than seven hundred of the strangest and most awe-inspiring places on the planet. Places motivate writers to tells stories, to give others information, or to share opinions in the forms of restaurant, hotel, and vacation destination reviews.

Thinking about a particular place may fill us with a sense of belonging or peace, or it may call up the sadness of loss or the joy of love. When we do not know what to write, we can always think about the actual physical places we have walked, biked, swam, slept, eaten, played, worked, laughed, cried.

TRY IT

Many years ago, I read *A Life in Hand: Creating the Illuminated Journal* (1991) by Hannah Hinchman. I carried it with me for a long time as it inspired me to deepen my own notebooking practice. One exercise Hinchman shares is how to take a "memory walk." For this, all you need to do is sketch a little walk, footsteps of your visit to a place you have once been. Then, along the walk, jot about what happened or what's important in each bit of the map.

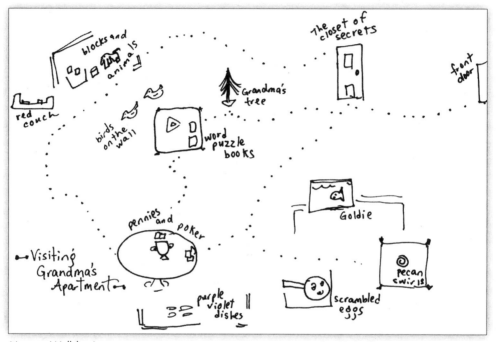

Memory Walk by Amy

You might introduce memory-walk-sketching as a regular practice for idea finding. Then, if students are ever idea-stuck, ask, "Have you tried taking a memory walk?"

Students can be inspired to write by place-related words such as "Grandma's Kitchen" or "Under the Tree," taking a little field trip of the mind. Or students might take a real field trip, writing in a new place together. Look around. Listen. You hear someone's far-off wind chimes and the rattling of cars on a Monday afternoon. There's construction going on in the distance, and these sounds are nothing like the sounds you'd hear at home. There, only birds.

Look through your classroom library or the school library for books and articles titled after places. Let these titles inspire poems or stories—take readers on tours. Tell why a place matters.

A Few Poetry Books Inspired by Places

- *Sacred Places* by Jane Yolen

- *Jumping Off Library Shelves; My America: A Poetry Atlas of the United States; Amazing Places;* and *City I Love* by Lee Bennett Hopkins

- *Dear Wandering Wildebeest, and Other Poems from the Waterhole* and *When the Sun Shines on Antarctica, and Other Poems About the Frozen Continent* by Irene Latham

STUDENT POEMS TO SHARE

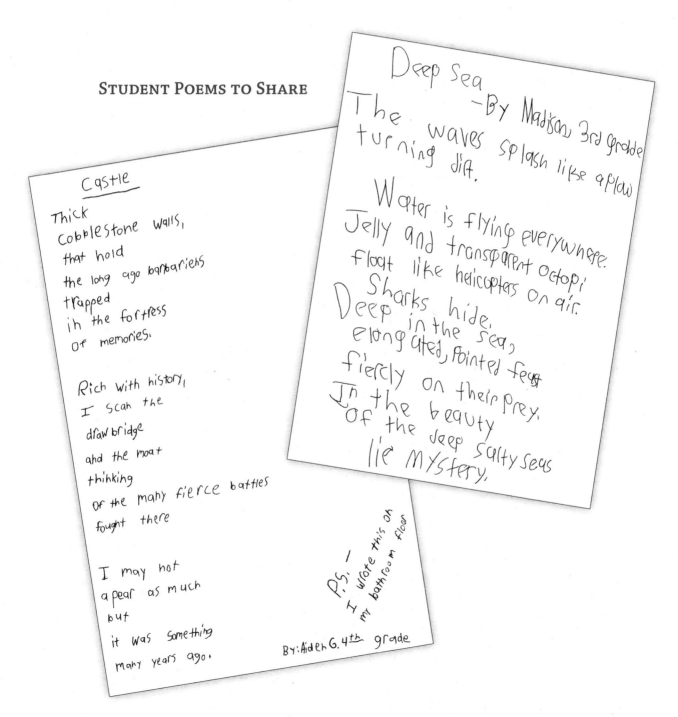

Castle

Thick
cobblestone walls,
that hold
the long ago barbariens
trapped
in the fortress
of memories.

Rich with history,
I scan the
draw bridge
and the moat
thinking
of the many fierce battles
fought there

I may not
apear as much
but
it was something
many years ago.

By: Aiden G. 4th grade

Deep Sea   -By Madison, 3rd grade
The waves splash like a plow
turning dirt.
Water is flying everywhere.
Jelly and transparent octopi
float like helicopters on air.
Sharks hide,
Deep in the sea,
elongated, pointed feet
fiercly on their prey.
In the beauty
of the deep salty seas
lie Mystery.

P.S. I wrote this on
my bathroom floor

Xenophobia

If you had xenophilia
and I had xenophobia
and we were from two cultures
far apart as night and day
then I would want to run from you
and you would want to run to me
and I would cry to look at you
and you would want to play.

Everything would frighten me.
Your different skin.
Your different prayer.
You would find me beautiful.
You'd reach your hand.
You'd try to share.

And I would hide inside my fears.
And I would tremble in my tears.
Such loneliness might last for years.

But you would still be there.

And one day I would look at you.
Your different prayer.
Your different skin.
I'd see your hand extended
and I'd know that we were kin.

I'd know you waited for me
with a love I did not earn.
It might take me a while
but eventually
I'd learn.

—*Amy Ludwig VanDerwater*

WORDS FROM THE POET

In April 2012, I took a "Dictionary Hike." Each day, I opened my dictionary to a new letter, A on the first and Z on the twenty-sixth of the month. Eyes closed, I pointed to a word on the page and then wrote a poem with that word as title. This was the poem for April 24, letter X, and I was delighted to learn the opposite of xenophobia. I believe we all can find inspiration anywhere and I regularly challenge myself to find ideas in thrift store bicycles, informational articles about glitter, and meters of popular songs. I choose to be inspired.

CONSIDER THE TECHNIQUE

These days I am reading *Pigeons: The Fascinating Saga of the World's Most Revered and Reviled Bird*. It's a book about the bird many call a "rat with wings," yet in the hands of pigeon-passionate author Andrew D. Blechman, these creatures are mysterious and beautiful. As we learned from *The Velveteen Rabbit* by Margery Williams, any subject can become fascinating, can come to life through the power of love.

Yet love doesn't just happen. We learn to love. Sometimes we even slog through love, acting kind when we do not feel kind. Most writers choose to write even when they are not in the mood to write, and many writers invent little projects to generate more writing.

On any given Friday, you can find poets sharing poems at their blogs as part of Poetry Friday. Readers can learn about how poets inspire themselves, find new favorite poems, and celebrate student poetry. During National Poetry Month, many poets share monthlong projects such as collections of poems about Pantone colors and audio clips (Laura Shovan), old family photographs and emotions (Mary Lee Hahn), art (Irene Latham), writing from mentors (Doraine Bennett), and the list goes on. With projects like these, poets assign themselves daily inspiration, and whether they feel like it or not, they write.

As I sit typing now, I occasionally pause to think and run my fingers through a small pile of smooth glass chips in pale blue, frosted clear, and green. I collected these last week at Sunset Bay Beach on Lake Erie, and I know that if I wished, I could write long about them. I might choose to write a story for each one, about the past lives of perfume bottle, medicine bottle, beer bottle. I could write about pollution or about art made from rubbish or about how beach glass reminds me of hard candy. I could make myself do this, and maybe I'd end up with something interesting. I can make myself write about any ol' thing, even a word I point to with my eyes closed. Because I believe that something will show up on the page, it does.

Writing can come from anything. Anything at all. Invent your own writing assignment, and complete it.

TRY IT

The work of finding ideas belongs to students. Instead of offering writing bandages such as, "Write about your puppy! You love your puppy," teach students to give themselves interesting assignments as writers. Here are a few places to get started, but encourage students to come up with their own ideas and share "What I Assigned Myself Today."

Listen to a poem or story read aloud. Write in the silence after listening.

- Read something to yourself and then write.

- Draw and then write.

- Pick a word and write.

Writing anxiety sometimes comes from fear that a topic will not be worthy, that there is no outline. Assure your students that beginning without a fully formed idea is a great way to begin, saying, "If you do not know what you are going to write about, you are lucky. Trust that an idea will come, and it will."

Years ago, my first-grade teacher friend kept a list of all the ways writers might self-inspire, titled "When You Don't Know What to Write." Illustrated with crayon drawings, the list included "Write from a word," "Talk to a friend," "Read a book to find an idea," "Look around the room," and so on. The list grew all year, and her students were never at a loss for how to begin.

Here's one last strategy for an I-don't-know-what-to-write moment. You can always borrow a line from a notebook entry, a favorite song, or a well-loved poem or book; copy this line; and write. Folks call this "lifting a line," and it works with all genres.

Sometimes I tell students how a black-capped chickadee will land on your hand if you hold out a palmful of sunflower seed, trust, and wait. Ideas are like these little birds. May they come to you.

Trees

It happens when you turn your head.

Trees tango
Trees tango
    cha cha
        do the twist.

You look back with a feeling
there is something you have missed.

Still and stately on their hill
quiet trees look down at you.

But when you look away from trees
they swing each other through the blue.

—*Amy Ludwig VanDerwater*

STUDENT POEMS TO SHARE

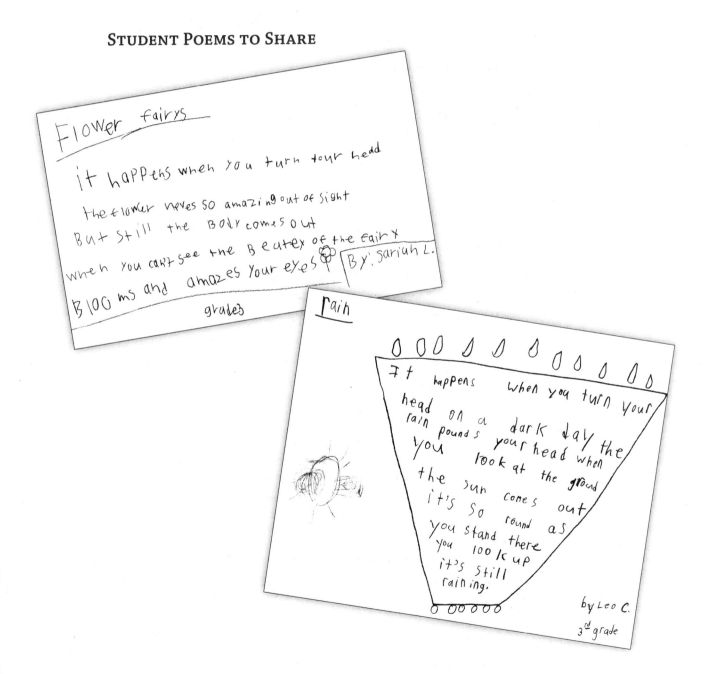

Flower fairys

it happens when you turn your hedd
the flower moves so amazing out of sight
But still the body comes out
when you can't see the Beutex of the fairy
Blooms and amazes your eyes

By: Sariah L.
grade3

rain

It happens when you turn your
head on a dark day the
rain pounds your head when
you look at the ground
the sun comes out
it's so round as
you stand there
you look up
it's still
raining.

by Leo C.
3rd grade

2
....

WRITERS CHOOSE PERSPECTIVE
AND POINT OF VIEW

In cities, we sigh in wonder over endlessly tall buildings and the bits of sky that thread them together. Yet as we walk beneath these skyscrapers, impressed by their enormity, people inside look down at us, and to them we appear as tiny ants. Perspective is all about where you stand.

Each writer chooses where to stand in relation to a subject. Be it poem or historical account, a writer asks, "Who will I be in this piece?" This decision sets the tone, inviting readers to see something from the inside out, or to live outside as a bystander looking into a new world. With stroke of pen or tap of key, a writer can turn a reader into a person who fears turtles or into a turtle itself. In this way, writers are magicians.

I recall school assignments that required a particular point of view, assignments like "Pretend you are a lost mitten and tell your story" or "Write a persuasive letter as the Thanksgiving turkey." These projects assigned both subject and point of view, so while I did experience playing with point of view, I never learned a why a writer might choose one perspective over another.

A writer's decisions are much like those spiral-bound books with different animal heads, torsos, and tails. A writer chooses a topic, then a point of view, then a structure—approaching subjects from different heights and windows. For example, if I write about my sister, I might write

- as my sister

- to my sister

- to you, Reader, who does not know my sister

- about sisters in general

In this way, changing perspective offers new writing possibilities.

Some writers choose unusual points of view, and some switch point of view or perspective, alternating between stances. For example, in this informational text, I speak from the *I* (first person singular), the *we* (first person plural), and the *you* (second person) point of view. I describe poets in a *he/she/they* (third person) voice. Doing so allows me to speak from my personal writing experience, our shared writing and teaching experience, and as an observer of other authors.

Learn to Choose Perspective and Point of View from Poems

Because poems are often short, readers quickly discover who is speaking and need only read a few lines to figure out the choice a poet has made regarding point of view. For example, in my poem "Trees" at the end of Chapter 1, you know from the very first line—"It happens when you turn your head"—that this poem addresses *you*, the reader.

In the same way we study themed poetry collections to learn about idea-finding, anthologies can also teach students about point of view. When a poet writes several poems around one subject, he will usually approach this subject from different angles. For example, in my book *Forest Has a Song*, I wrote the poem "Warning" in a second-person *you* voice, warning readers of possible itchiness. On the other hand, I wrote "Fossil" in a first person voice, sharing a memory of a fossil coming to life in my hand: "I dug in the creek bed. . . ."

Sometimes a text surprises readers with its unusual perspective, as this poem does, written from a poem's point of view.

Word Wanted

POEM seeking just the right word.
Must dazzle when written, spoken, or heard.

Slight words, trite words need not apply.
Precise and concise words, give us a try.

Regardless of your part of speech,
a noteworthy job could be within reach.

Endowed with sound second to none?
Potential for growth if you are *the one*.

—*Robyn Hood Black*

Who is the speaker in Robyn Hood Black's poem? What is the situation? Why might she have chosen as she did? Conversations about such choices inform exploring writers.

Invite students to write several poems or notebook entries about the same subject, but from different points of view. You're writing about dogs? Be the dog begging at the table. Now be the child. Now the mom. Now a bystander. Now a dog owner giving advice to a reader about how to raise a puppy. Speak to the mom. Speak to the dog. Which works best?

Enjoy thinking about point of view in the pages that follow. Consider the alternate choices these poets could have made. How would Lee Wardlaw's mask poem about a taco have been different in third person? How would Jack Prelutsky's poem have felt different in first person?

Bilingual

Because I speak Spanish
I can listen to *Abuelita*'s tales
and say *familia, madre, amor.*
Because I speak English
I can learn from my teacher
and say "I love school!"

Because I am bilingual
I can read books and *libros*,
I have friends and *amigos*,
I enjoy songs and *canciones*,
games and *juegos*,
and I have twice as much fun.

And some day,
because I speak two languages
I will be able to do twice as many things,
help twice as many people
and do, everything I do, twice as well.

Bilingüe

Porque hablo español,
puedo escuchar los cuentos de mi abuelita,
y decir *familia, madre, amor.*
Porque hablo inglés
puedo aprender de mi maestra
y decir *I love school!*

Porque soy bilingüe
puedo leer libros y *books*,
tengo amigos y *friends*,
disfruto canciones y *songs*,
juegos y *games*,
y me divierto el doble.

Y algún día
porque sé hablar dos idiomas
podré hacer el doble de cosas,
ayudar al doble de personas
y hacer todo lo que haga el doble de bien.

—*Alma Flor Ada*

WORDS FROM THE POET

While I find inspiration all around me, much of my writing is the direct result of my own reflections and memories. An example is my childhood memoirs, Island Treasures: Growing Up in Cuba. *While now published as a volume, it is the compilation of writings done over a long time.*

For me, as a reader, I find first person produces an immediacy that reaches in a powerful way: "Here is the author baring her soul and sharing it with me." Of course, for this to happen, the writing must be sincere. Being bilingual has been a most defining aspect of my life. In fact the title of my memoir for adults is Vivir en dos idiomas (Living in Two Languages), *so it is only natural that I would share with children what the privilege of having two languages has meant for me, with examples that could relate to them.*

CONSIDER THE TECHNIQUE

The first person singular—*I* voice—in a poem or other text creates a relationship between writer and reader. First person is, well, *personal,* and it gives us the sense that we know the writer, that we may be friends. This perspective creates a feeling of camaraderie, a feeling of, as Alma Flor Ada writes, "immediacy."

In her poem "Bilingual/Bilingüe," Ada poetically lists what she describes as "a most defining aspect of my life." She uses the pronoun *I* to guide and frame her words; she is gently "baring her soul" to us.

Writers often choose a first person singular voice to create a feeling of relationship. In narrative works, such as Jacqueline Woodson's *Each Kindness* (2012), Chloe speaks in her own voice straight to readers. She knows us, and she confides in us, sharing story and regret. Had Woodson written *Each Kindness* in third person, we would stand apart from Chloe's feelings. Consider the difference between these two sentences, one directly from the text and the other with a shifted point-of-view. The first feels as if we're being pulled close, and the second feels as if we are removed from Chloe.

> *First person: "When I reached the pond, my throat filled with all the things I wished I would have said to Maya."*

> *Third person: "When she reached the pond, her throat filled with all the things she wished she could have said to Maya."*

Sometimes writers avoid first person so as not to interfere with subject matter. News reporters, for example, sharing impartial information about events, write in third person. Writers of feature articles, on the other hand, may insert their *I* voices as a crafting tool. Opinion pieces are often written in first person, and writers who write regular columns create ongoing relationships with readers. Week after week, as they share thoughts with us we feel that we are part of these writers' lives.

By exploring the pronoun *I*, this humble one letter word, we help students understand one powerful perspective possibility.

TRY IT

Use notebooks as a place to experiment with first person writing. In *Lessons That Change Writers* (2002), Nancie Atwell invites students to keep lists of "writing territories," areas of expertise and interest, topics they can return to over a lifetime. I keep such lists in my notebooks, and as Alma Flor Ada asks herself, you can ask your students, "What are the most defining aspect of my life?"

Poet George Ella Lyon is well known for her poem "Where I'm From," a list poem written in first person singular, detailing her personal history. (Read this poem at Lyon's website: www.georgeellalyon.com/where.html.) To play with first person, have students write "Where I'm From" poems of their own. Press further, asking each to choose one line and to write a new poem from this lifted line. Return to these in later units of information or opinion or narrative, lifting lines again.

Where I'm From

I am from late-night laughter.
From Mean Girls and Grease.
I am from roses in my backyard
(pink and lovely, they smell like sugar).

I am from books full of stories
From Percy Jackson to The Fault in our Stars.
I am from 300 page comics,
From finishing them in a week.

I am from practicing long hours at gymnastics.
From pull ups that numbed my arms.

I am from baseball caps and dutch braids.
From sticky-sweet frappuccinos and macchiatos.

I am from a world where I am told
what to do.
From "don't do this," and "don't do that."
I am from a world where I am told
what I am.
From "No, you're a girl," to "No, you're not good enough."

I am from a variety of music,
from Macklemore to One Direction.

I am from week long vacations,
From jack fruit to lychees.

I am from a small town in the United States
with parents born in a different country.

I am from all of these moments.
Each like a drop of water,
letting me thrive.

By Lauren C
grade 7

For personal narratives and personal essays, your students will naturally write in the first person singular voice, but you might invite them to write their fiction in first person, allowing them to become the characters they write about.

Make point of view a regular part of reading discussions. Ask, "How would this story be different if the point of view were changed?"

Writers might choose the first person singular voice when they wish to

- tell a true story from their lives

- tell a story from the perspective of a character

- create an intimacy and a relationship with readers

- share opinions

STUDENT POEMS TO SHARE

My Superpower

It's nearly nighttime
I stay out when the sun sets
And then I freeze time
To watch the sunset
I wait until snow comes here
And then time begin
I am the time queen
I have other powers though
Like making cold ice

By: Yhaerstin D.
Grade 5

Memory Poem

Crisp, colorful pages
Sprinkled with words and pictures.
Carefully, craftily,
Weaving a web of tales.

I lean in, captivated
Slowly wrapping my brain around
A summarized life.

Our 16th president,
Always honest,
Slave abolishing,
What? Dead?!

No!

Eyes watering, welling, overflowing,
Sniffles turn to sobs
I can't stop the waterworks!

Everyone's staring at me!
Head down,
Eyes closed,
Pretend that you are invisible.
Hovering teachers, buzzing busily.
Chiding other kids for laughing.
I storm out.
I just want to go home.
PULL YOURSELF TOGETHER!
Deep breath, calm and collected.

by Katherine D.
grade 8

Miracle in the Collection Plate

Rev. Christopher Rush, 1850

Brothers and sisters, we know why we're here
this evening. The sad news has traveled fast
of Brother James's capture. For three years
he lived amongst us, tasting happiness.

His wife and child are here with us tonight.
God bless you, Sister. Without a goodbye,
James was handcuffed, and shoved on a steamboat
to Baltimore, to be sold—legally!

Neighbors, we know that upright, decent man:
James Hamlet: a loving husband, father, friend.
Many of us would gladly risk the fine
or prison sentence, if we could help him.

My friends, all is not lost! It's not too late!
We are told that Brother James may be redeemed!
His buyer will sell him! But we cannot wait:
we need eight hundred dollars to free him.

Eight hundred. I know every penny counts,
living from widow's mite to widow's mite.
But with God's help, we can raise that enormous amount!
Let's make a miracle in the collection plate!

—*Marilyn Nelson*

WORDS FROM THE POET

This is a persona poem, a dramatic monologue in which the speaker (the "persona") is speaking to a meeting at the church he pastors. Since he is addressing a group, he refers to the gathering in the first person plural we.

Creating a scene to tell the true story of the 1850 capture of James Hamlet as a result of the Fugitive Slave Act enacted that year by the U.S. Congress seemed to be the best way to convey the drama of the situation and the combined power of the small amounts of money that members of the free African American community were able to donate to purchase James Hamlet's freedom. Scenes and speeches like this one happened hundreds or thousands of times in African American churches around the country between 1850 and the present, as the African American community was exhorted to stand together to fight racism and the powers of oppression. In a dramatic monologue such as this, the speaker's voice describes or implies the scene and the group included in the we.

CONSIDER THE TECHNIQUE

First person plural point of view—*we*—shares a sense of immediacy and intimacy with first person singular—*I*. Occasionally, a writer may tell a story that belongs to a group and choose the first person plural because it seems right for the story. For example, in the picture books *Shortcut* and *Bigmama's*, Donald Crews writes mostly in first person plural when sharing group adventures.

Sometimes, the first person plural point of view—*we*—includes the reader. An author may choose this perspective to make clear that speaker and reader are in a particular situation together and they share something, in the case of Marilyn Nelson's poem, a desire to free James. Had Nelson written her poem in third person, introducing Reverend Rush as *he* and the congregation as *they*, readers would experience the story as onlookers rather than as insiders. Her choice of point of view brings this scene to life on the page and in our hearts.

Sometimes in life, we must write a letter or an email on behalf of a family, professional organization, or other group. In such cases, we choose the first person plural point of view to indicate that the writing comes from the group we represent as well as from us.

We can be a positive, reaching out, inclusive word. Opinion writers may invoke the first person plural voice as a way of connecting with an audience, presuming that readers agree with them. Speechwriters often use the *we* voice to include listeners in a message, to make clear the ways we are alike. But *we* can also be exclusive and off-putting, especially when the reader does not see himself as part of this *we*. It can create an "us against them" mentality—sometimes seen in political speeches—and this can be dangerous. Part of the Declaration of Independence reads, "We hold these truths to be self-evident, that all men are created equal, that they are endowed by their Creator with certain unalienable Rights, that among these are Life, Liberty and the pursuit of Happiness." *We* was an interesting pronoun choice here as its antecedent did not actually refer to everyone in this country, but only white, landholding men. By selecting first person plural point of view, an author may create community for the good of all or for the good of one group alone.

Writers might choose the first person plural when they wish to

- tell a personal story that includes more than one protagonist

- create closeness with an audience by including them in a collective *we*

- create division between groups by speaking in *we* against *they*, *us* against *them* terms

TRY IT

Your students may not have thought about first person plural point of view, so read a few texts that employ this perspective. Show students how some narratives, some stories, such as Crews' *Shortcut* and *Bigmama's*, are told from the *we* point of view, as a way of sharing a story that belongs to a group. Ask them to think about stories that they share with others, stories that might be more truly told from the *we* than the *I* voice. For example, I would write my memories of riding in the "wayback" of our family station wagon in the *we* voice because these memories are completely tied to my relationship with my little sister, Heidi.

Sometimes, in nonnarrative pieces such as letters or speeches, a writer will employ the first person plural *we* voice. In studying such texts, ask your students to discuss these questions:

- Whom is the speaker including in the *we*? Is the *we* inclusive or exclusive?

- Is the speaker part of the community addressed?

- Is the speaker trying to convince readers/listeners of something or implying more of a relationship than exists?

Invite your students to experiment with the *we* point of view in notebooks, writing in the *we* voice to communities they are truly part of or to fictional or historical communities. It is important to remember, though, that authors do not generally make choices in this way. Authors do not sit and say, "Today I will write in the first person plural." Point of view, especially in nonfiction, is often simply a natural selection based on genre, purpose, and audience, but as with anything, things that come naturally often come with practice first.

The Books

Have you ever wondered
what it's like to be a book?
We are always getting thrown around.

People drop us,
rip off our pages,
tear off our covers.

Yeah, it's a hard-knock life.
All we do is sit on shelves,
hoping and praying
someone will come
and take us home.

When someone comes
to check us out of the library,
it's like a vacation
Whether we go to a big house,
or a small house,
it really doesn't matter.

All that matters
is that someone
cares for us
                by Logan Q.
                grade 6

Baseball Players

We are the baseball players
We love the sound of the ball hitting the bat
And the sound of our cleats hitting the base
Going for a home run

We love the sound of our parents cheering us on when
we are up next
And when we win the sound of our hands slapping
eachother saying
Good game
Good game

        By: Emily O.
        grade 5

Alphabet Stew

Words can be stuffy, as sticky as glue,
but words can be tutored to tickle you too,
to rumble and tumble and tingle and sing,
to buzz like a bumblebee, coil like a spring.

Juggle their letters and jumble their sounds,
swirl them in circles and stack them in mounds,
Twist them and tease them and turn them about,
Teach them to dance upside down, inside out.

Make mighty words whisper and tiny words roar
In ways no one ever had thought of before;
Cook an improbable alphabet stew,
and words will reveal little secrets to you.

    —Jack Prelutsky

WORDS FROM THE POET

*I frequently write in the second person because it makes a direct connection with the reader. In the case of "Alphabet Stew," I wanted to encourage the reader to experiment with words—*you *can do this: play with words to produce surprising results. By twisting sounds and meanings, and making new combinations out of them, a poet can make words "reveal little secrets."*

CONSIDER THE TECHNIQUE

Jack Prelutsky's "direct connection with the reader" is what second person is all about. Second person is the *you* voice, with speaker addressing reader head on. This point of view creates either an instant bond or a disconnect, and a writer who chooses second person stares into a reader's eyes whether the reader likes it or not. Find a funny example of this point of view in the introduction to Georgia Bragg's informational book *How They Croaked: The Awful Ends of the Awfully Famous* (2012): "So here's a warning: take care of yourself, the world, and everybody in it. But if you don't have the guts for gore, DO NOT READ THIS BOOK" (vi). While this historical book is written in third person, the introduction speaks directly to the reader, in a second person *you* voice.

Since *you* is the stated or implied subject in a second person text, when writers choose this perspective they are, in effect, telling readers what to think and do. This might feel friendly—or bossy. Prelutsky's second person *you* voice in "Alphabet Stew" is bouncy and inviting, but sometimes the *you* voice oversteps, annoying or angering readers. Long ago, I read a novel written completely in second person. I was disconcerted as I read of the affair I was having with an Italian stranger.

Students will be familiar with second person if they have read the Choose Your Own Adventure novels in which readers select various paths. "If you choose to open the closet door, turn to page 74. If you choose to turn back, turn to page 81." The readers—*you*—are there.

Informational authors use this voice too. The If You historical books, including *If You Traveled West on a Covered Wagon* by Ellen Levine, drop readers into various time periods. Chapters ask questions such as, "How did you make the buffalo meat last a long time?" Similarly, Judy Allen and Tudor Humphries have written a series of second person science picture books, including *Are You a Snail?* and *Are You a Ladybug?* These books help readers imagine living as different creatures.

The second person *you* voice can transform a reader's experience in a way that third person cannot. Certainly, an author can describe preserving buffalo meat or give a detailed account of how a snail moves, but to actually make the reader feel as if he is doing these things makes reading a near virtual-reality experience. Like magic, an author turns readers into pioneers or ladybugs.

Look for the second person voice in do-it-yourself books in which authors whisper, "Here's a tip for you," into the ears of makers and chefs. Procedural texts such as these use the second person voice to help readers follow directions easily and to make the teacher feel close by.

Writers of opinion sometimes employ second person point of view, imploring political leaders in personal letters, giving speeches in support of or against causes.

Prelutsky invites us to allow words to "reveal little secrets" to us. One of these secrets is that point of view affects readers—it affects *you*.

Writers might choose second person when they wish to

- inspire readers to try something

- teach readers

- transform readers into something or someone else

- speak directly to readers, asking for help or expressing an opinion

TRY IT

Take time to examine a few texts written in the second person, asking students to discuss why an author may have selected this stance rather than first person *I* or third person *he/she/they*. What does the second person voice lend to the text—a sense of relationship, a conversational tone, an opportunity for a reader to momentarily live a different life?

Welcome students into the world of second person writing by asking them to list any of the following:

- subjects about which they feel qualified to give advice

- adventures and experiences they wish to invite others to try

- difficulties they have experienced

- places they know well

- hobbies and interests they could teach

Have students select a topic from any one of these lists and experiment in their notebooks with the second person *you*. They may choose to write in prose—or in poetry, as Prelutsky does with "Alphabet Soup." Share. How does it feel to write from this place? When might you choose to write in second person?

In social studies or science, students might write brief pieces in second person, modeling short texts after the If You history books or Are You science books. These exercises need not be long or published, but can allow young writers the opportunity to try on this writing stance. And always, notice writers' addressing readers directly as *you* whenever you encounter it in texts, connecting your students' writing with their reading.

STUDENT POEMS TO SHARE

Those words

Those words you shot at me
penetrated
like a bullet
and crushed my heart.

A big, dark cloud
washed through my body.
It hurt.

But, all you could see
Were my warm, salty tears
hitting the ground.

by: Owen L.
grade 6

Book
Take a book
that's it pick it up
gain the knowledge
the power
the power you could make stronger
not by the internet.
not by wizards books.
not by magic
but by you
Take a book
that's it pick up
open it
gain power

By: Jessenya L.
Grade 5

Solitary

Sunk
as if
in a well
no one
remembers
the convict
whose eyes
have forgotten
sun
whose feet
have forgotten
earth
knows only
one light:
he did
not do
it.

—*George Ella Lyon*

WORDS FROM THE POET

My poem-path didn't start off in third person the day I began "Solitary." It went through second person:

> let yourself down   word hold by word hold
> listen to the earth breathing

to first person, written from inside a well:

> a cave of poems I will never see
> so I listen for their voices

back to second person:

> If you fell
> in a well

and then a question in first person:

> what wants me to say it

Then the beginning of the poem:

> Sunk
> as if
> in a well . . .

I chronicle this journey to show that I didn't consciously decide to write in third person. I felt my way toward it. I played with possibilities.

With those lines, the voice took hold for me and led me to discover who the poem was about.

As a citizen, I'm horrified by our huge prison population, by privately owned prisons that profit from this, and by the huge percentage of prisoners who are black. Around the time I wrote "Solitary," I heard an interview with a man who had been wrongly imprisoned for decades and was finally out. Writing in third person let me imagine—make images—for his suffering without claiming it, as a first person narration would do.

CONSIDER THE TECHNIQUE

A writer may choose to stand somewhat apart from a subject, for reasons of distance, accuracy, or honesty by writing in the third person *he/she/they* point of view. In third person, a writer creates a bit of space between self and subject, does not claim to live in the world of the subject, and does not directly address readers.

Third person point of view is an observational stance. In fiction, a writer may use this point of view to create a sense of omniscience, in which the speaker observes and knows everything happening, including the inner feelings of all the characters. Or, more commonly, the writer may limit the third person point of view to just a single character.

For her poem "Solitary," George Ella Lyon explains, "Writing in third person let me imagine—make images—for his suffering without claiming it, as a first person narration would do." Lyon keeps herself a bit apart, honoring that this is not her story. Rather, it is the story of one particular man, the convict, *he*.

Our students know this point of view. It is the point of view of fiction, of Elizabeth Bram's *Rufus the Writer* and Gary Paulsen's *The Monument*, stories that allow readers to look into others' lives. This is the voice of "Long, long ago . . ." and it is a contemporary stance too. Picture books and novels and poems written in third person cast a spell of other-time-and-place, allowing readers to experience new worlds without entering them as actors.

Third person is also the objective, unbiased voice of news reporting in which a writer observes and reports with impartiality. Writers of fake news have capitalized on this—making something untrue sound true by using tools of strong news reporting, including the objective third person voice.

The third person point of view can even mask personal narratives. By choosing to recast real-life material as fiction, a writer can keep her personal issues private, giving them instead to an invented character. This is a decision a writer makes: "Where will I stand in this piece?" Of course, as with any writing decision, the choice to write in third person is not always a conscious one. Lyon explains, "I felt my way toward it. I played with possibilities."

Writers might choose third person when they wish to

- tell a story about characters, sharing the imagined inner thoughts and feelings of each
- tell a story about another person, standing apart
- remain impartial to the subject when reporting news
- write about their own struggles or issues without sharing personal information

TRY IT

When your students write personal narratives, they pay attention to the daily events of their lives. To help them explore writing in third person, ask your students to tell the story of another person—from the outside. If they are writing fiction, have them imagine their characters' thoughts. And if they are writing about real people, as Lyon was moved to write from hearing an interview, encourage them to simply bear witness to the small actions they see and the words they hear. Reading poems such as "After Work" (2002) by Richard Jones or "Splitting an Order" (2009) by Ted Kooser helps me understand others' lives through poets' eyes. Have your students try writing poems like these.

To discover multiple points of view, focusing on the third person, give older students newspapers and invite them to read for point of view. Ask, "What do you notice on the front page? Editorial page? Sports page?" Discuss independent reading books, focusing on differences between books written in first person and third person. How would a book read differently if the point of view were changed? Try rewriting a few sentences of a class read-aloud, shifting the point of view, and then talk about the difference.

Keeping a consistent point of view is a challenge for many writers. When students write fiction, for example, they often slip from the third person *he/she/they* to the first person *I* voice. Young fiction authors often write fiction about personal memories, changing only a smidge here or there, or they are so deep in the writing that they actually feel that these scenes *are* happening to them. Teach students to reread their writing, listening to be sure that the point of view remains consistent unless a shifting point-of-view is intentional.

STUDENT POEMS TO SHARE

Great-Horned Owl

Whoosh!
This dangerous predator
Stares intently into his prey's
Trembling face,
Its hook-like beak
With a slick chestnut body
And haunted eyes.
His message is clear:
        Beware.

                Lola K.
                Grade 3

My Best friend

She is beautiful
Her hair is glossy and black
She is my best friend
Her cheeks are blushing
Her lips are red like roses
Her eyes are shiny
Her skin is soft and luscious
She is caring and kind
And she makes me laugh everyday

                Marshae, Age 9
                Grade 4

History Lesson

Deep in the blue-gray belly
of *Sierra Madre*
I was born.
I heard tell that
paper scraps
—not pancaked corn—
served as my folded shell;
Black powder,
the story told,
the spicy *carne*
around which I was rolled.
Then calloused fingers,
quick and deft,
plugged me
into chiseled clefts
of tunneled stone—
and lit me afire!
With spit and sizzle,
flame and flash
my blast
produced a thunderous groan
and confetti rain of rock
and ore . . .

My name?
Taco de mineros
—miners' taco—
and I fed the *hombres*' hunger
for silver wealth
and fame.

—*Lee Wardlaw*

Sierra Madre (see-ER-uh MAH-dray): mother mountains.
The *Sierra Madre Occidental* is a major mountain range in western Mexico;
the range is home to some of the richest silver mines in the world.

carne (KAR-nay): meat or beef

taco de mineros (TAH-ko day mee-NAY-rohs): miner's taco
Small charges, similar to miniature sticks of dynamite, were used by eighteenth-
century silver miners to excavate rock.

hombres (OHM-brays): men

WORDS FROM THE POET

Tacos are my favorite food. History, my favorite subject. So I loved researching the when, how, and why of tacos. Knowing an object's backstory helps bring it to life, helps the writer step inside that life and speak about it as one's own. Ordinary transforms into deliciously extraordinary—like tacos. In this poem, I express a taco's boastful pride for the role it played in Mexico's mining history: I'm more than lunch—I helped create an industry! Stepping inside an object, writing as the object, helps both poet and reader understand what it wants or needs, how it feels—and why.

CONSIDER THE TECHNIQUE

Poems written in the voice of another person, an animal, or an object are called *persona* or *mask poems*. The voice is first person singular (*I*) or first person plural (*we*), but the speaker is not the author or a traditional character. In a persona or mask poem, the author is *other*—a praying mantis, a toaster, a pebble.

In "History Lesson," Lee Wardlaw writes as a taco teaching us about its heritage. We feel as if we are gathered 'round, listening to a relative, and for a moment all tacos are alive. We suspend our disbelief in talking tacos. We pay attention.

It is a good exercise to imagine life from someone or something else's point of view. Wardlaw is not a taco, but in pretending to be one—in wearing a taco mask—she sees life through a taco's imagined eyes and she widens her own understanding of tacos and the world.

Many informational authors write in other personas. In *Significant Studies for Second Grade* (2004), Karen Ruzzo and Mary Anne Sacco detail an informational writing unit focused on local birds. Each student selects one bird to research through reading and expert visits. Then, after studying mentor texts written in first person, books such as Jim Nail's *Whose Tracks Are These?*, each student publishes a small bird book, written in the *I* voice of the bird studied. Many writers of information use this technique, and in magazines such as *Ranger Rick* and *Big Backyard*, students will find authors writing in other personas, wearing a variety of masks.

Wardlaw explains, "Stepping inside an object, writing *as* the object, helps both poet and reader understand what it wants or needs, how it feels—and why."

Writers might choose to write through a mask, or in a different persona, when they wish to

- set a whimsical tone, allowing readers to experience an unusual speaker

- help readers understand the experience of an animal or object from the inside out

- create a sense of empathy or understanding for a subject
- give readers an opportunity to hear the voice of a person from the past or from afar

TRY IT

For our youngest students, pretending to be something other than oneself is not difficult. Games of dress-up and farm and spaceship prepare children for writing in the voices of trees and shoes, doctors and mermen. Ask your students to remember and share pretending stories, and invite them to turn these memories into simple mask or persona poems or other texts.

You might ask students to list names of people or animals or objects they find fascinating, chose one, and then try writing in its voice. As they write, encourage them to consider what this particular person, animal, or object "wants or needs, how it feels—and why," as Wardlaw has done, by asking questions such as

- Who and what does it/she/he love?
- What does it/she/he fear?
- Why might it/she/he want to write to your readers?
- What matters most to it/her/him?
- What might readers learn from it/her/him?

Depending on your current content-area unit, students might use science or social studies research to write poems, informational texts, or persuasive texts in other voices. Students writing multigenre pieces might place a persona or mask poem alongside an informational text about the same subject. Ask, "What does the mask piece add to the published work?"

In an opinion unit, take the advice of *Writing to Persuade* (2008) author Karen Caine asking students to write as a person who holds a viewpoint different from their own. Students may even hear a stretching sound in their brains and hearts as they pretend to believe things they do not believe. But after such an exercise, students will likely have a newfound appreciation for something they may once have considered "ridiculous" or "just wrong." Talk about this.

Pretend, pretend, pretend. This is an important muscle for all writers to develop. As we strengthen our abilities to see the world from multiple points of view, each leaf, each mouse, each stranger, becomes important and worthy of our attention and care.

Little Leaf

I am a leaf
and I die in fall.
My home gives oxygen
and I love spring.
Caterpillars eat me
I change colors during seasons
spring is coming back
did you miss me?

Shayna6.Grade 2

Sky

Yes I am the sky,
bright blue,
dark blue,
I see clouds,
planes and
helicopters.
I see night and day,
day and night I stay awake ...

by Karl M.
grade 3

Great Blue

Heron
stretch your great blue
wings out to catch the sun.
Cast a shadow on the surface
so that

you can
see beyond the
glistening reflection
into the moving shade beneath.
Heron

stretch your
great blue neck so
you might see a meal swim
by near the surface of the creek.
Pick up

one leg,
move it slowly,
slowly, slowly, until
with calculated speed your great
blue beak

snatches
unsuspecting
fish for lunch at the creek.
Then heron lift your great blue wings
and fly.

—*Doraine Bennett*

WORDS FROM THE POET

When speaking directly to something or someone in a poem, the poet makes a connection, almost like talking with a friend. You can say things to a friend that you might not say to someone else. That freedom to speak helps me bring the subject to life. It often helps me see things that I might miss otherwise.

CONSIDER THE TECHNIQUE

In an apostrophe poem or poem of address, a writer speaks to a person, animal, or object in direct address. In "Great Blue," Doraine Bennett speaks straight to a heron, brings it into the room of her poem, and we readers suddenly inhabit this heron-room too. We recognize the second person *you* voice, but the difference here is that this *you* is not *you the reader*. Rather, it is someone or something specifically identified by the writer: a family member, an elected official, or even a heron. Readers become eavesdroppers, listening as an author speaks to this other, not-present person or animal or object. Bennett describes this as making a "connection, almost like talking with a friend."

On any given day, we speak to people and objects who are not actually listening or cannot even hear. We yell at athletes on television, and we call, "Keys! Where are you, keys?" This is natural, and students will think of many examples in which they or others speak to objects and people, present or not. Here it is in writing—apostrophe poems or poems of address.

Columnists sometimes use this technique of address. Certainly, we write to others when sending actual letters or emails, but sometimes a writer will share a letter to a specific person publicly, considering two audiences at once. In "A Letter to a Son on His 18th Birthday" (2000), Leonard Pitts writes to his own son, Marlon, but by publishing the memoir-like letter in the newspaper, he stretches his audience beyond one father and son to all parents and children.

In the same way, in January 2017 Barbara and Jenna Bush addressed an open letter in *Time* magazine to Malia and Sasha Obama as the Obama family prepared to leave the White House. This letter describes the lives and struggles of First Children, and while providing personal support to these two newest members of the former First Children club, it also speaks to the rest of us, showing us how difficult it is to be a First Child: "You have listened to harsh criticism of your parents by people who had never even met them." The letter shows support for one audience (the Obama girls) while it educates another (the public).

Writers might choose to write directly to a subject when they wish to

- praise something or someone or someplace
- share an opinion with one particular person and, at the same time, with a greater audience, with either the same or different intentions for each
- criticize openly

TRY IT

If your students have experimented with writing mask or persona poems, invite them to open their notebooks to those pages. Ask them to use the same lists and notes but try speaking *to* their subjects rather than *as* their subjects. Then have them place their two finished drafts—persona/mask and apostrophe/direct address—side by side. Give students time to read each other's text pairs on the same subject and to talk about what they notice and admire in the writing. Which do they prefer? Why?

Consider having students choose someone from a current news story, a public official, or a celebrity of interest and write to this person, either in poem or letter form. This writing may actually be intended for the person addressed—or not. Similarly, you might ask students to list issues that trouble them and to address related people or groups of people in writing, highlighting these concerns. Encourage them to write to large groups ("Dear Parents Who Yell at Coaches") instead of individuals ("Dear Mom") to keep personal issues personal and to address a larger audience.

For joyous writing, ask students to celebrate favorite places and objects and people—from snowmobile to teapot—by writing *to* them in odes or poems of appreciation. Afterward, experiment with turning these poems into letters or opinion pieces that celebrate the virtues and strengths of their subjects.

Writing is like a reversible jacket. You can take a poem and turn it inside out into an essay, or you can take a mask poem and turn it inside out into a poem of address.

Alarm Clock

oh clock oh clock
why do you tic toc?
why do you make
those loud ringing sounds
in the early morning?
why do you have hands?
if you do you should have
arms and legs and a head too
be considerate
let me sleep
you should have ears to hear your
screams!   by Leo B. grade 2

Guitar

Guitar
How I wish my fingers could slide
across your many frets and strings
to create beautiful music.

Guitar
Why can't I play
the mushy "a" chord?

And why can't I create
perfect harmonies and melodies?

Why don't they blend together
with the lyrics I sing
and notes that go with them?

By: Laura S., Grade 7

3

WRITERS STRUCTURE TEXTS

If you build a new home, your friend will ask, "What is the floor plan?" You will answer with details about your soon-to-be ranch, center entrance colonial, or geodesic dome, and your friend will easily envision the structure of your home-to-be. We have house-shape pictures in our minds. So it is with writing.

Like houses, excepting perhaps the Winchester Mystery House, most texts have observable structures, and young writers benefit from learning to analyze how pieces of writing are constructed. When reading a novel, we notice whether it moves straight through time or flips between past and present. When reading an article, we pay attention to whether it is structured through time, by comparison, or as a list. In the same way, when we read a poem and ask, "How do the parts fit together?" we help our students understand how poetry structures mirror the structures of other genres.

Some writers plan and follow blueprints like architects; others let a structure emerge. And just as a homeowner may call a builder with a change, a writer may alter a text's organization while drafting or revising. But regardless of how a piece is written, writers benefit from studying its structure.

I once attended a workshop in which the leader explained that every piece of writing can be seen as a story or a list. Consider patriotic songs. "The Star-Spangled Banner" tells a story moving through time with a clear beginning, middle, and end. We (first person plural) battle through the night, but at the end our flag remains. On the other hand, "America the Beautiful" moves through a list of several American strengths, praising our purple mountains and pilgrim feet, with a repeating refrain requesting grace. We can find these two organizational structures—story and list—in everything we read and write. Of any text, we ask, "Is this a story or list—or some of both?"

Authors compose stories and lists in different ways, and the patterns we find in texts offer possible structures for our own writing ideas. Studying structure, a writer realizes that her *idea* about fish can be shaped as a *story* about a time she went ice fishing or it can be shaped as a *list* of reasons to protect waterways. She can now write either a narrative or an opinion draft, each organized differently. Experimenting with various structures can push ideas into new territory too. Our fishergirl, drafting an informational how-to-fishing guide, will think in different ways, challenged by an informational structure. Many authors live off of the land of one or two topics for life, reshaping their favorite subjects in different containers of genre and form.

An understanding of structure and organization grows from reading and talking about writing architecture. Sometimes we skip structure study, instead turning to premade graphic organizers that feed us for only one day. To feed writers for more than one writing day, we can teach them to "read like writers," as Katie Wood Ray describes in *Wondrous Words* (1999), learning ways to shape and plan ideas across a writing life.

Learn to Structure Texts from Poems

With their few lines, poems simplify structure study. The first stanza of Arlene Mandell's poem "Little Girl Grown" (2001) begins on Monday—"Monday I tied blue ribbons in her hair"—moves through other days of the week, finally ending on Sunday, when the little girl is all grown up and has moved away with her fiancé. Similarly, in Ed Young's *Seven Blind Mice*, a retelling of an Indian tale, each page explains what a different mouse saw on each day of the week. This poem and picture book, along with many other texts, share a days-of-the-week structure, and in a poem, we recognize this without turning a page.

Structure, organization, helps us know where we are going as writers. For readers, structure offers comfort—readers can count on the builder of this piece to shape a house that makes sense. When we study structure through poems, we teach our students to see how a story poem is like a personal narrative, how a poem with two parts is similar to a magazine article that compares and contrasts. Before long, students begin to recognize, "We know a poem shaped like this book. We know a poem shaped like this essay. We've seen this architecture in poems—let's bring it to prose."

Margo

I helped Margo
    with buttons in second grade,
    skating and soccer in third,
    explained jokes over and over
    so Margo could laugh, too.
    Margo, slower than the rest of us,
    counted on me to wait,
    to help her catch up.
    Depended on me
    to pull her along,
    to help her belong.

Now I see Margo
    at the edge of a crowd,
    looking more than lost.
    She doesn't see me wave.
    We're in different classes,
    I'm going places
    Margo can't find.
    Margo. Margo
    falling farther
    and farther
    behind.

—*Kristine O'Connell George*

WORDS FROM THE POET

Picture stanzas as drawers in a bureau. Similar or related items are stored in each drawer. In "Margo," the first "drawer" or stanza gives examples of how things used to be. In the second stanza, the reader learns how things are right now. Now, peek at one of your poems: What is in your stanzas?

CONSIDER THE TECHNIQUE

Stanzas are, in a way, the paragraphs of poems. When we look at a poem from afar, we can easily determine where stanzas begin and end. Some poems are only one stanza long, but poems are often built from several stanzas. Young readers can count and identify stanzas even if they cannot read. To do so, we simply find the white space, and count the chunks of words between them. Kristine O'Connell George's poem "Margo" is two stanzas long.

George's image of stanzas as "drawers in a bureau" is a perfect way to describe the function of stanzas—or of paragraphs. We place like with like, and we separate these chunks of meaning with space—with a whole white line in between each stanza of poetry or with five indented spaces before a new paragraph in prose. The two distinct stanzas in "Margo" make a before and after instantly clear. With poetry, stanza shapes often hold meaning.

Poets and prose writers begin new stanzas and paragraphs when they wish to

- allow a new speaker to speak

- move to a new topic

- signal a change in location

- indicate passage of time

- mark a change or contrast

- highlight an important word or phrase

- build and sustain a repeating pattern

- create a certain sound or rhythm

Readers like visual signposts along the reading path, and in the informal Latin of classical times, *stanza* meant "stopping place." Readers need words. And readers need pauses too, pauses between ideas, speakers, new subjects, new thoughts. Should you wish for a cup of tea, you know you can get one in a moment, right at the end of this paragraph. Now.

TRY IT

Show your students how stanzas appear on a page: as blocks of text separated by white space lines. Compare stanzas to paragraphs, indicated by white spaces at the beginning of each new paragraph. Both stanzas and paragraphs separate ideas, speakers, thoughts, perspectives. To help students study stanzas, ask partners to read a small collection of poems, either a typed packet or poetry book, discussing what they notice about stanzas. They can address these questions:

- When does the poet decide to begin each new stanza?

- What do you notice about the number of lines in each stanza?

- Is each stanza the same length? If not, why may they be different?

Students will be familiar with the sound of stanzas from songs. You might print out the lyrics of a popular song for stanza study. Note that the chorus is a repeating stanza and that each verse is its own stanza. Should the song have a bridge, this too is a new stanza.

Invite students to reshape a short piece of their own writing (any genre) into a poem with stanzas. Model choosing a page or paragraph, and show students how you might break it into stanzas. Or try this with the words of authors your students know, asking them to turn bits of fiction and nonfiction into poems with stanzas, changing not words, but only layout. Display these found poems along with the original texts, asking writers to explain how they decided when and where to begin new stanzas. Then try this exercise again with the same text, but with different stanza breaks. How do stanza choices affect a reader?

As you teach your students about stanzas, highlight the connection to paragraphs. Poets and prose writers alike must decide which sections of writing belong together and which should be separated from each other. We place them in "drawers" called stanzas and paragraphs.

Summer,
Shouts,
Schools out,
And the sun blares out.

Summer,
Fun,
Sailing in the sun,

Summer,
Struggle,
Beginning of fall trouble

Summer,
Gone,
Fast, Not long.

By: JC L.
Jones
Grade 7

Joy

Joy is a flickering
light that could go
out at any time.

One second - yay!
Your lights on
but the next moment
you're sad and your
lights out.

Everyone has
a light in
their body,
somewhere, waiting
to be turned on.

Or, if they're
not sad or joyful,
it's flickering,
waiting for their light
to turn on or off.

Christian Z.
Grade 3

I don't think I'll ever get used to

walking home from school	alone
playing Madden	alone
listening to Lil Wayne	alone
going to the library	alone
shooting free throws	alone
watching ESPN	alone
eating doughnuts	alone
saying my prayers	alone

now that Jordan's in love
and Dad's living in a hospital

—*Kwame Alexander*

WORDS FROM THE POET

I begin a list poem with a topic and a collection of connected articles or concepts. First, I brainstorm a list of topics. Once I select a topic, I list words and phrases about the subject, things surprising or unusual to make the poem more interesting. The more ideas I produce at this point, the more material I have to work with when drafting. As the number of ideas grows, I am forced to employ divergent thinking, and this leads to more unique list poems. List poetry is meant to make unusual connections, and often such poems end with an important message for the reader by offering a piece of advice, ending with the most unusual concept, closing with something funny, or repeating the first line (adapted from Alexander and Colderley 2015).

CONSIDER THE TECHNIQUE

Life is full of lists. We jot lists of things to do and lists of groceries to buy. We laugh at funny "Top Ten" lists and scribble lists of possible dog or baby names. Lists are usually long and skinny, and we can spot one right away. Our students make and use lists too, from summer camp packing lists to baseball teammates. In school, students see various bulleted lists, from lunch menus to homework planners.

We find lists in many genres. The nonfiction books *1,000 Places to See Before You Die* by Patricia Schultz and *The 7 Habits of Highly Effective People* by Stephen R. Covey are each written in a list structure. Some listy texts have numbers in the title, and some, like Judi K. Beach's picture book *Names for Snow*, do not.

Unlike a story, a list need not be ordered by time. To draft in this structure, a writer may first list a group of related objects, people, thoughts, questions. You can list anything: colors, countries outlawing the death penalty, cat breeds, reasons to detest Jell-O. In an article or essay, the down-the-page list shape will likely vanish into prose paragraphs detailing each list entry, but an attentive reader will still note the list shape.

Texts written in a list format, regardless of genre, usually end with a change. Many teachers affectionately call this a "list with a twist." In Kwame Alexander's poem, we feel a punch in the gut at the end, due to the loss of the repeated word *alone* and the heartbreaking reasons for the speaker's aloneness. In his persuasive and informational list book *Reading Makes You Feel Good*, Todd Parr celebrates the gifts of reading, including learning, imagining, and more, ending with the pattern-breaking line "And you can do it anywhere!"

From baby board books (counting books, color books) to dissertations about invasive species, to letters to the editor regarding traffic problems, lists are everywhere. A list structure says, "These things go together," and once familiar with this organizational pattern, writers will likely anticipate and experiment with their own listy pieces.

TRY IT

To experiment with a list structure, tell students they can begin with any topic—insects in the park, a favorite school subject, an idea they feel strongly about. Subjects are infinite. Ask students to write a list—or a few lists—related to their topics, and when their lists feel ready, teach them to turn the lists into poems. Line breaks in a list poem are are easy to determine as each line usually introduces a new part of the list, but ordering a poem requires some decisions. Sometimes a list will be arranged in a particular way, such as farm animals from smallest to largest or band instruments by section. Sometimes a writer determines order by listening to the rhythm of words. Some lists feel randomly ordered. Encourage students to order the lines of their list poems in different ways; suggest that they read the lines aloud to choose which order sounds best. Study list poems from books such as Georgia Heard's *Falling Down the Page* and Elaine Magliaro's *Things to Do,* and discuss how poets order their lists.

Help your students think about the endings of their list poems. Show them how to introduce something new or make a statement in the last line, breaking the list pattern and signaling that the poem is finished. Students might try several surprise endings to see which best matches the moods they hope to create.

Keep your eyes open for list structures when you read aloud in various genres, and invite students to find texts you can add to a growing "collection of listy texts." Consider writing list poems at the end of content-area units, giving students the opportunity to synthesize their learning and wonders in a different way. Or turn short list poems into long articles of information or opinion, elaborating on each line in a genre switch.

Average Morning

Bright lights
Thrown covers
Dirty clothes
TV blasting
Shower running
Dark sky
Cold floors
Warm waffles
Loud crunching
Tired People
Paper bags
Backpacks zipping
cars roaring
Friends appear
Bikes clicking
Just an average

Morning

By: Ryan R. Grade 7

What to eat if you want to be a Runner

Some
things
you should
eat are...

Fish,
Chicken,
Turkey
Beets,
Eggs,
Beans,
Yogurt,
Cheese,
Pack a lot
of protein.

Clara W.
Grade 3

My Heart

It was the biggest,
most beautiful Valentine.
Sitting in fifth grade
we watched Ms. Hernandez
cut and paste cardboard,
ribbons and lace to create
a work of art—a giant heart
with curly ribbons
that sprang back when
she pulled on them.

The words *"Be Mine"*
winked and smiled
from its lovely face.
We touched the pretty lace
with our fingertips.

Every day I'd lift my eyes
to that heart, wishing
for it, not for myself,
but for *mi mami*.
She would know
just how much I loved her
if I got straight A's
and won it for her.

On February 14th,
Dia de San Valentin,
Ms. Hernandez,
shook a pink satin box
in the air—a treasure chest.

I cupped my hands,
put my head down,
and prayed deep inside.
I prayed from the very heart
of my heart—I prayed
from *mi corazón*.

Suddenly, the whole class
clapped. I lifted my head.
Mrs. Hernandez' eyes shone.
"Lupita," she read my name
from the red ticket in her hand
and smiled, softly, sweetly.

On wobbly legs,
like a clumsy toad,
I stumbled out of my desk
to receive my prize.
It was a miracle.
I was sure of it.

That afternoon
I traipsed home
with that huge, red heart
tucked safely under my arm.
It slapped against my leg,
stroked my ankle,
and scraped the ground.
That's how big it was—
my love.

—*Guadalupe Garcia McCall*

© 2018 by Amy Ludwig VanDerwater, from *Poems Are Teachers*. Portsmouth, NH: Heinemann.

WORDS FROM THE POET

"My Heart" illustrates something that happened to me a long time ago, when I was very young. The story comes from a very important event in my life, a memorable moment, something I don't think I will ever forget. Memories are a great place to find stories, and because they are so vivid and brief we can use these special moments in our lives to write a narrative poem (a poem that tells a story). By focusing on the structure of a narrative (beginning, middle, end) we have the story, but by using imagery (specifically the five senses) we have a visual story in the form of a poem.

CONSIDER THE TECHNIQUE

Narrative is the central way that humans communicate. We tell stories to connect, prove points, remember. And a strong story includes more than actions, more than a list of, "I did this . . . then I did this. . . ."

Story writing is a bit like baking a cake. When mixing cake batter, it is not enough to simply dump flour, flour, and more flour into a bowl. Cakes also need butter, sugar, and baking powder. Stories need varied ingredients too: actions, dialogue, thoughts and feelings, and descriptions. And all you need to write a strong prose story can be found in the small space of a story poem.

Stories include actions, and Guadalupe Garcia McCall captures a wide range of actions small and large that help readers see and *feel* what's happening. Look at the physical actions she captures—clapping, head lifting, eyes shining, reading and smiling.

Stories include dialogue. In McCall's poem, we hear Mrs. Hernandez's voice read "Lupita" aloud. Letting the teacher speak rather than saying what she said ("Mrs. Hernandez called my name") brings her voice to life. We readers hear her words.

Stories include characters' thoughts and feelings. In "My Heart," we are privy to the speaker's secret wish and silent prayer, not because she speaks it aloud, but because she tells what is in her mind.

Finally, stories include visual and sensory descriptions. McCall describes "a giant heart / with curly ribbons / that sprang back when / she pulled on them." Descriptions help readers leave reality and live inside the story. Descriptions help us know how fluffy and chubby Grandpa's guinea pig is, help us reach up to touch the flaking paint on a bedroom wall.

It is important for students and writers of all genres to tell stories well. For not only does storytelling enrich our lives and deepen our wisdom, but when we can tell pointed stories, these stories can serve all of our writing, whether we wish to entertain, teach, or persuade. In *Minds Made for Stories* (2014), Thomas Newkirk asserts, "We don't read extended texts through sheer grit, but we are carried along by some pattern the writer creates. Even if our goal is to learn information, we don't do that well if that information is not connected in some way—and as humans the connection we crave is narrative" (18). In other words, humans want stories.

TRY IT

Build your students' internal sense of story by saturating them in story. You might tell a story each morning, but instead of saying, "Oh gosh, I almost hit a deer on the way to school today!" slow the story down. "Students. This morning, as I looked out at frost tipping the grass, my breath making chilly clouds in my car, I saw something out of the corner of my eye. I wondered what it was and said. . . ." Or, as Martha Horn and Mary Ellen Giacobbe and recommend in their book *Talking, Drawing, Writing* (2007), you might create a daily ritual where students tell their stories in this same way, paying attention to the elements of good storytelling (actions, dialogue, thoughts and feelings, and description) as they share.

To help understand the sequence of stories, students can use timelines to think through a series of story events, or they can imagine these events across the pages of a blank book, thinking about what happened first, next, at the end.

Encourage students to weave together the elements of story by asking them to fold their papers in half and then in half again, labeling each quadrant with a heading: actions, dialogue, thoughts and feelings, description. From this brainstorm sheet, students can write story poems with line breaks or stories in booklets, braiding action with dialogue with feelings with description.

Through repeated and joyous storytelling, your students will learn to go beyond action-lists, in their poems, in their long narratives, and in storybits sprinkled into opinion and informational texts.

Magic Ride

Something big and bright
crashed down on me.
I pushed it off
and inspected.
A hot-air balloon
was now mine.

I climbed into the basket
not caring
about where I was going
or how I would steer.
I just let the wind take me.

It was amazing
to fly so high.
I could gaze upon
everything.
I felt the wind rush
through my hair.
The balloon flew up high
then dropped me through
the roof of the building.

There were no floors.
The building rested
on a cloud.
Shelves of books
lined the walls.

It was a library.
There were other balloons,
but I was the only
person here
in this magic library.
The destination of
my magic ride.

By: Meghana V
Grade 6

Feather

red bird fLying
got
ina Fight
feather
came
off
red
bird
Went
home

Braden m.
3rd grade

See Saw

I'm up!
I grip—
my feet are dangling

        I'm down!
        I bump—
        my bones are jangling

I'm up!
I push—
my back is straight

        I'm down!
        I press—
        my legs take weight

It's not that far
from up

        to down—

the sky stays blue

        the dirt's still brown

What I see
and what I saw

        follows all of
        nature's laws

but when I'm up
the things I see

        and when I'm down
        the *way* I see

feels
wholly different

        to me

—*Heidi Mordhorst*

WORDS FROM THE POET

This poem explores the view from two different positions, two different perspectives. Back and forth, one voice contrasts the view from the top of the seesaw with the view from the bottom. These two positions are rather close in space, but the feeling of hanging up in the air versus bumping down on the ground turns out to be very different! When we zoom in closely to capture the specific details of two places or voices or opinions in a poem, suddenly the similarities—or maybe the differences—pop out, and then we understand something new about the world.

CONSIDER THE TECHNIQUE

I remember riding the seesaw with my sister. When I was up, I swung my legs in sky. When I was down, I held my feet on earth. Up. Down. Up. Down. Two sets of feelings. Middle school was much the same.

A back and forth structure allows a writer to compare and contrast, and we find it in various genres: alternating between settings, characters, and points of view in fiction; or ideas, opinions, and subjects in nonfiction. Kate Messner employs this structure in her picture books *Up in the Garden and Down in the Dirt* and *Over and Under the Snow*. We recognize it in the hit song "Summer Nights" from *Grease* as Sandy and Danny sing different versions of the same date. We know this structure from Gary Paulsen's *Canyons*, with voices and time periods alternating between a modern-day boy and the Native American boy whose skull he finds. This structure feels like a Ping-Pong game:

- your turn / my turn / your turn / my turn

- alligators / crocodiles / alligators / crocodiles

- past / present / past / present

With this structure, an author weaves two lists together, like interlacing fingers, and then she often ends the piece by breaking the pattern, bringing together the ideas, providing a deeper insight into—or playful treatment of—the subject at hand.

In Heidi Mordhorst's poem, we follow her seesaw journey back and forth, and we experience how she feels when up and down. This structure helps writers show how two subjects are alike and different, deciding which aspects of each to highlight. It's also rhythmic, allowing readers to anticipate the next voice or time period or topic. At times, the formatting of a text highlights the back and forth nature with different fonts, italics, or indenting. Poems for two voices, such as the ones in Paul Fleischman's *Joyful Noise*, make this back and forth structure visible.

TRY IT

This structure is easy to spot and fun to try. Begin by making two parallel lists about two different people or places or time periods or two anythings at all. You might begin with notebook entries or with content such as historical figures or scientific wonders, whatever you wish. Here's an example:

Child Wearing a Pair of Sneakers	**Child Making a Pair of Sneakers**
On a basketball court	In a factory
Proud of my sneaks	Tired of working
Listening to parents cheering	Listening to machines clattering
Dreaming of winning	Dreaming of going to school
Eight years old	Eight years old

See how I could turn these two lists into a simple seesaw poem without too much trouble? Or, if I prefer, I could use this same structure to write an information/opinion book, alternating between a child who wears sneakers for basketball and a child who works in a factory, making those same sneakers.

Encourage students to write back and forth free verse poems and to reshape them as articles or essays. Help them see how a back and forth poem about two types of animals could be reshaped as an informational article in the voices of the two, each teaching about habitat, parenting styles, and diet.

In *But How Do You Teach Writing?* (2008), Barry Lane shares a poem format he calls a "lullaby weave," which alternates lines of an already existing song with lines of a personal narrative. Such a simple technique can yield profound poetry and make this structure clear.

Do's and Don'ts
to
Be in miss.corgill's Class.

Do: learn how to colaborate.
Don't: Be a bully.
Do: Be an upstander.
Don't: act CRaZY.
Do: be yourself
Don't: be mean (we will work it out.)
Do: learn from mistakes
Don't: have a bad attitude.
Do: be curious.
Don't: say someone is wierd.
Do: be a thinker.
Do: be Determined.
Do: be courageous.
Do: be a hard worker.
Do: grow.
Do: be a teacher.
Do: be a lot a lot of other things.

by Moira D.
grade 3

Dogs

Dogs are mans best friend
they are always there.
Listening in, even if they don't care.

Woof! Woof! I bark,
danger ahead, watchout for the door,
someone may break in.

My dog looks out for me
through good times and bad,
always ready to comfort me when I am sad.

Woof! Woof! Belly rubs ahead
thanks, that tickles, I love them before bed.
Comforting you, with licks to the face,
I love hearing your laugh when you shove me away.

Night has fallen, and by my side,
my dog is there, always prepared.
Watching out for danger, though having fun too.

Woof! Woof! Bed time has arrived,
I jump into bed,
on high alert,
to protect my best friend.
I love my human and he loves me too,
I can't think of anything better to do.

By: Mia K.
Grade 6

Soccer Sides

Offense means head down the field—
dribble,

          pass,

                    try to score!

Goalie blocked your shot?
No sweat!
Follow up and shoot some more!

                    Defense means hang out in back.
                    Better keep a watchful eye!
                    Their offense wants the winning goal—

                        Ha!—
                        I'd like to see them try . . .

          —Matt Forrest Esenwine

WORDS FROM THE POET

I was driving home from an indoor soccer game I'd just played and was thinking about opposite sides, differing viewpoints, and "Soccer Sides" came together. I wanted to show the two sides of a team while also showing the two teams' opposite goals (that is, desires); I also wanted to add a surprise by revealing the speaker is actually in *the game! The poem's action and rhythm required some creative enjambment, too, to underscore the energy of the game itself.*

CONSIDER THE TECHNIQUE

Organizing text by building two sides is another way to show how two things are alike or different. The difference is that instead of rocking back and forth, back and forth, a writer stays back, back, and then moves forth, forth. Here, a reader feels less movement between ideas, focusing attention first all on one subject (or idea, opinion, time period, and so on) and then moving to the second. In essays, some call this the block method: a block of text about living with Mom followed by a block of text about living with Dad.

Children will know picture books that illustrate this structure. Charlotte Zolotow's *When I Have a Little Boy / When I Have a Little Girl* can be opened from front or back, with one side listing how the speaker would raise a boy child and the other listing how the speaker would raise a girl child. And Arthur Howard's *When I Was Five* is also divided into two sections. In the first half of Howard's book, the five-year-old speaker shares some of his favorite things—a future career, a car, a dinosaur. Then we read a change page, "Now I'm Six," after which he shares his new favorites, now that he's a year older. The ending breaks the pattern, surprising readers with the same favorite friend at both ages—Mark.

In his poem, Matt Forrest Esenwine visibly delineates the difference between offense and defense on a soccer field, dedicating the first two stanzas of his poem to offense and the second two to defense. In the same way, Kristine O'Connell George's poem "Margo" (found on page 85) is split into two halves, each describing the same child, but at two different times.

There are many ways to explore different subjects with this two-sided structure. I might explore the difference between living in the country and living in town, for example, or my life before children and my life after children.

The website diffen.com allows readers to insert two subjects for comparison and then generates a text comparing the two, describing one in the first half of the document and the other in the second half. Once again, we find a structure in our poetry reading that can ripple out into different genres.

TRY IT

To compare and contrast by building two sides, you may begin with some of the same lists and exercises from the previous lesson about weaving back and forth. Using "Soccer Sides" as a model, remind students of Esenwine's words: "I was driving home from an indoor soccer game I'd just played and was thinking about opposite sides, differing viewpoints." Challenge students to think of places or times in their own lives in which they notice two sides or two viewpoints: sports rivals, opinions on cell phones for children, living in a bilingual home.

Young narrative writers might experiment with this structure by writing about one idea from two points of view, perhaps writing the first point of view in one color, switching in the middle, and then writing the second point of view in a different color. After this exercise, talk about what writing from two points of view does for a writer—and for a reader.

Using a book like *When I Was Five* as a model, you might ask students to remember personal life changes. Have them each make two lists, one about life before the change and one about life after it. From these two lists, they can write notebook entries or poems or other pieces. Thinking about life before and after dog ownership, for example, might inspire an essay about the importance of pets or a nonfiction book about dog care. Regardless of whether students publish their two-sides explorations, working with ideas in this way will help students recognize a compare and contrast structure in the wild.

Sisters

Sisters are hard to explain...
Sometimes they fight with you.
And later forgive you.
They can sometimes give you
A hard time.

And Say, "You're being mean."
And, "Stop acting like that."
But sometimes they're
nice.

They stand up for you.
and share a piece of
their Valentines candy,
And sometimes when it's raining
They let you come under
the umbrella.
Sisters are Sisters.

by: Ella G.
grade 3

Differences

A church on every
corner
Tall buildings
aparments and
parks

Cars honking
sirens going by
traffic traffic
traffic

Warm beaches and
Suger white sand
painted houses and
Pretty Gates
delicious ackee
family family
family

By: Zada P.
Grade 5

At the Carnival

Who beeps his horn in a hearty hello?
"Me," says car. "Hop in! Let's go!"

Who sails the sea or floats on a lake?
"Me," says boat. "Ahoy, young mate!"

Who rides the track with a clackity click?
"Me," says train. "All board now, quick!"

Who cruises high in blue summer sky?
"Me," says plane. "Whoopie! Let's fly!"

Who rides cars, boats, trains and planes?
"Me," says Child. "May I do it again?"

—Heidi Bee Roemer

WORDS FROM THE POET

When writing in a question and answer structure, first I pick a topic. I may imagine a conversation between animals or objects. What would two hippos say? What would Worm ask Robin? Or Hammer ask Nail? My poem may ask who, what, when, where, why, *and* how. *The tone may be serious or amusing.*

CONSIDER THE TECHNIQUE

Just as nesting dolls fit one into another, many structures fit inside other structures. The question and answer structure is a specific type of back and forth structure, and it is also a list. Many informational texts are organized through questions and answers, for example *Why? The Best Ever Question and Answer Book About Nature, Science, and the World Around You* by Catherine Ripley. We see this way of organizing text in magazines, in which it is used to structure complete articles or sidebars, as well as Q&A guides like the spay/neuter pamphlets in veterinarians' offices, and newspaper advice columns about parenting, home repair, or etiquette.

Fiction can organize itself around questions and answers too. In Barbara M. Joose's picture book *Mama, Do You Love Me?*, a little girl poses a series of questions to her mother. Does she love her? How much? Would her mother love her if she acted in a variety of naughty ways? After each question, mother reassures child that, yes, she loves her dearly and will forever, no matter how naughty she is.

A question and answer text may have a serious or lively tone. Consider Heidi Bee Roemer's "At the Carnival." Roemer could have chosen to simply list carnival rides and explain what each does. But by beginning each couplet with "Who . . . ," she lightheartedly transforms these vehicles into characters, gives them voices, and perks up our ears as we wonder, "Who *does* 'ride the track with a clackity click?'" In her whimsical picture books *Who Hops?* and *Who Hoots?*, Katie Davis plays with questions and answers too.

The strength of this structure lies in its straightforwardness. It is simple to recognize and try. One need not think about transition words, and the order of questions often does not matter. Sometimes, question and answer texts have leads or conclusions that frame them; sometimes they don't. Roemer ends her list of questions and answers with a child's voice after a series of talking vehicles. Pattern broken—poem complete.

Writers use a variation of this structure when they pose one single question and follow it with many answers. Wonderopolis.org, the popular classroom website featuring one daily question and answer, is built around this organizational pattern. One new day, one new question, one new answer. List picture books such as Rebecca Kai Dotlich's *What Is Square?* (1999) and articles like "Ready for College? Why Some Students Are Prepared More Than Others" by Lisa Heffernan (2016) pose one question and then answer it in many ways.

TRY IT

Using Roemer's poem as a model, invite students to try writing in a question and answer structure by choosing familiar subjects from their own interests or from old notebook entries, art, or a content area. Model turning information into questions, just as contestants on the TV quiz show *Jeopardy!* do, creating simple question and answer poems or books or thinking in notebooks. To learn more about writing question and answer books, see chapter 3 of *First Grade Writers* (2005) by Stephanie Parsons. While Parsons' book is written for teachers of first grade, the ideas in her nonfiction chapter are useful for older writers too.

For ongoing practice with this structure, regularly ask students to each write one question and one answer about a topic of study, bringing these together into class publications. This practice doesn't take long, gives students a chance to synthesize content information, and builds up a great collection of community-written picture books or articles about the subjects you study throughout a year.

Teaching your students that questions and answers can structure a complete text will give them one more possible map for writing today—and forever.

Q+A interview

Hi there miss, what's your name?

It's miss Lauretta Dane

Tell me, when did Columbus sail the ocean blue?

In 1492

What's a word that starts with a P like Pentagon?

Um, Parthenon!

Tell me something about VanGogh!

When painting Starry Night, he really let go

What about aboats lifesavers?

During emergencies, they're often our saviors,

Well, that's all, thank you very much!

If you'll excuse me now, I must eat my lunch!

By Ada B

Grade 6

Night Time At The Park

Who's walking
down the street?
"me" says the human
Saying goodbye.
Who's that
Playing with knit?
"me" says the cat
rolling around with it.
Who's that at the park?
"me" says the kid
going down the slide.
Who's that in the tree?
"me" says the bird
going to sleep.

Written By Shayna M.

Grade 2

How to walk around the block

Wear shoes.
If they have laces, make sure they are tied.
Pick a direction and go.
Double foot hop
over sidewalk cracks,
then stop and pick up a rock.
No snooping in your neighbor's mailbox
(You'll get in trouble if you get caught.)
Woof bark woof bark woof bark woof;
ask before you pet that dog.
That stick could use a new location.
Remember,
where you started is your destination.
'Cause 'round the block
is a circle
(even if it is really a square).
Arriving back at your front door,
you'll be a different person
when you get home.

—*Michael Salinger*

WORDS FROM THE POET

Poetry and pattern are intertwined. Poems are a perfect vehicle to teach procedure, which is just another pattern of steps—beginning, middle, and end. In my poem I knew the start and finish point (my front door). My job was to answer the "what happens next" that occurred sequentially in between.

CONSIDER THE TECHNIQUE

Directions may be seriously informational or they may be fanciful, as we discover in Michael Salinger's poem "How to walk around the block." But regardless of slant or intent, the structure of procedural writing includes the same elements: how-to holds a reader by the hand and guides. And yes, directions are a special, organized form of list. Salinger explains, "Poetry and pattern are intertwined. Poems are a perfect vehicle to teach procedure, which is just another pattern of steps—beginning, middle, and end."

Instructions are everywhere. Last night, my fourteen-year-old researched indoor soccer drills as I followed a recipe for lasagna. And while direction-writing primarily takes the form of informational text, this way of organizing can also apply to humor, as it does in Delia Ephron's *How to Eat Like a Child, and Other Lessons in Not Being a Grown-Up* or in articles like the one I found on wiki-How titled "How to Take Your Pet Rock Camping."

The structure of procedural writing is clear in Salinger's "How to walk around the block." First, the poem might easily be written as a numbered list of actions, sequenced from beginning to end. Start to finish, line by line, we learn what to do, and how. Along the way, Salinger anticipates where readers might make mistakes and warns them ahead of time: "No snooping" and be sure to "ask before you pet that dog." He also seems to know what we are thinking, answering our unspoken questions in parentheses. Procedural writers must imagine, "What will my readers need to know? What might they wonder? How can I help them understand these risks and steps?"

Some procedural texts include introductions or lists of things a doer needs, and they often include a "Why?" usually at the beginning or end. (Remember the list with a twist from earlier in this chapter?) Salinger offers this at the poem's end as he closes with a promise: if we take a walk, even just around the block, we will be changed. This, the reason behind the instructions, is the part that makes me want to take a walk. The poem's final twist motivates a couch potato to stand up.

Sequencing and braiding these instructional parts—ingredients, clear steps, warnings, answers to anticipated questions, and bits of motivation—are what writers of directions do. In poems—and in prose.

TRY IT

Most people enjoy teaching others how to do things. Knowing how to ride a bike, fold a napkin a fancy way, write computer code—these skills are a source of pride, and sharing instructions not only can be informative to learners but can be exciting for those sharing them as well.

Play a new game, make a new craft, or cook a dish with your class. Then write a how-to—maybe in prose, maybe as a poem—with all the important parts. In terms of structure, help students see that each line or paragraph break might be a new instruction. Writing a how-to can be a useful exploration of both clear directions and clear text breaks.

Students might also keep a notebook page listing things they know how to do:

- crafts they can make

- dishes they can cook

- problems they know how to solve

- building or repair tasks they can explain

- procedures involving animals or plants

- things they do regularly that make life good (I bet Salinger likes walking!)

And of course, students can have great fun writing procedural texts with a spin, books written in different viewpoints or in silly ways, such as Susan Pearson's picture book *How to Teach a Slug to Read* or any of Sally Lloyd Jones' how-to series books, including *How to Be a Baby, by Me, the Big Sister.*

Sleding

It snowed
out
hooray
have a snack
have a drink
get
on our
gear
time
to
go
sleding
get to the top of the hill
hooray time to go down!
weeeeeeeeeeeeeee

Connor M.
grade 3

How to Sleep

first put on your pj's
get in bed
Put Cover's on
Breathein andout
Get comfy
close youreyes
Dream pleasantDreams
And now you can SLEEP!

by James Q.
grade 3

Caterpillar Dreams

In the emerald dew of morning,
the plump caterpillar
nibbles her final leaf,

reaches a willow twig,
hangs upside down,
a tiny acrobat.

In the crystal quiet
August afternoon,
she spins her silky cocoon

and weaves her evening dreams
into a satin quilt
of silver wings.

—*Charles Ghigna*

WORDS FROM THE POET

The cycle of time has been a popular subject of poetry throughout history. In this poem, I wanted to show the magical cycle of the caterpillar as she quietly transforms into a beautiful butterfly. As a backdrop to the caterpillar's three cycles, I chose the three times of day: morning, noon, and night.

CONSIDER THE TECHNIQUE

Our days are regulated by time: times of day, days of the week, months of the year, years past and future. We keep track of what we have done and what we will do by calendar, watch, or cell phone, and we easily talk about events because we share the same units of measuring time. We can organize texts this way too.

Eric Carle is famous for organizing picture books through standard units of time. *The Grouchy Ladybug* marches through times of day, hour by hour, with little clocks drawn on every page. *The Very Hungry Caterpillar* brings readers through a week of eating, Monday through Sunday. Form follows function, and often a writer will use the function of time to structure writing. As readers, this can be a comfort. When reading a book organized by months, we enjoy predicting that January will be followed by February.

Many prose pieces are structured through units of time. Child development articles and books walk parents through monthly and yearly stages, and articles such as "Gardening Through the Seasons" by Lou Bendrick (2010) lead us through seasons, offering tips on how to garden all year long. Even cookbooks can be organized through time, as is Victor-Antoine d'Avila-Latourrette's *Twelve Months of Monastery Soups* (1989).

Years ago, after I wrote a lice poem for Lee Bennett Hopkins' anthology *Nasty Bugs*, our family got lice. When the ordeal ended (and my science teacher husband finally put the microscope away), I decided to make something from it. As I pondered how to organize my essay, *The Very Hungry Caterpillar* came to mind—days of the week. Hence, my second person local radio commentary "A Week of Lice" (on my website). The piece was a snap to write because the road of Monday (when the lice note comes home from school) through Sunday (when I vowed not to read any notes from school) helped me plan.

All stories move through time, but in these examples, time is made visible. In texts structured through time, hours, days, months, or years are named with words or shown in pictures of clocks or calendars or headings, and the movement of time is part of the plot. In Charles Ghigna's "Caterpillar Dreams," readers understand that morning turns to afternoon turns to evening as a caterpillar begins its journey to butterfly. This is how life goes.

TRY IT

Teach students that, just as they can melt water from rectangular ice cube trays and pour that same water into spherical ice cube trays or trays shaped like stars, they can play with structure, superimposing the organizer of *time* onto a subject they have already written about in a different way. A lost hamster story can roll out hour by hour and an election op-ed can play out month by month.

Invite your students to look through notebooks or folders, choose a topic they've already written about, and pour it into some new mold of time, such as

- hours of the day
- days of the week
- months or seasons of the year
- years in a particular timeline

Help your students see how structuring writing through time looks on the page. A week-poem, for example, may have seven lines or stanzas, or a year-article may comprise twelve paragraphs.

During the time I wrote these words, our bright red kitchen clock stopped, and honestly, I feel a bit lost. Time helps us find our place, in our days and in our reading. We can use these time templates to plan our written texts.

Time
Gone

When I
was three

I met
my grandmother

She's a shining
blessing that
made my three
year old heart
bloom

When I was
seven I visited
her in Africa

She taught
me how to
have an african
soul

When I was
nine she visited
America

I taught her
how to have
an american soul

Now I'm ten
and she's dead
her soul awaits
for me in heaven...

By: Mercy T.
Grade 4

Seasons of My Basketball Hoop

In Fall
Children run around
And fling orange balls at you.
Every time the ball hits
It makes a starliting rattle
And animals run away.

In Winter
You are under a huge blanket
Covered in white
As you watch children playing in the snow.
You watch white flakes come down
And wait for Spring.

In Spring
The laughter of children
Fills the air.
You watch them
Shooting lacrosse balls,
And you wait patiently
Enjoying the sunny air.

In Summer
When all the kids are out of school
And are playing with you once again,
You love the company,
But hate the arguments.

by Danny L.
grade 6

Overnight at Grandma's

red
—the railing on the stairs up to Grandma's apartment
orange
—the sunset in her kitchen window
yellow
—sugar cookies
green
—my mom's bike in a framed picture
   from when she was eight
blue
—the ocean in the old book
   with the story about a brave girl
   whose brothers were turned into swans
violet
—the hand-knitted blanket my grandma tucked around me
   when I fell asleep on the couch

   —Susan Marie Swanson

WORDS FROM THE POET

We are surrounded by patterns: night and day, questions and answers, the cycle of the seasons, the beating of our hearts. I love watching for patterns in the world and in the poetry that I read, and these patterns help me generate and organize my thoughts and my words. The structure of this poem came from the rainbow, a sequence of colors that is always the same, but which can describe an endless array of experiences.

CONSIDER THE TECHNIQUE

As Susan Marie Swanson says, our world is full of processes and patterns, most of which follow cycles, some of which we can see. Many children have witnessed a chick hatching from its shell, and many more have rejoiced at a peek of bean plant poking its head through well-watered soil. The moon becomes small and then becomes big again. We watch ocean waves sigh in and out, in and out.

In "Overnight at Grandma's," Swanson selected the colors of the rainbow to carry her readers through a warm visit to a loved one, coupling this with a pattern of time, beginning with arrival and ending with sleep. Natural patterns are reassuring for readers. We enjoy reading Swanson's words, knowing that after "orange" will come "yellow" followed by "green." We know how rainbows go, and this structure will not surprise us. Rather, it will offer a new way to see Grandma's, a fresh way to take a visit to a favorite place.

Informational text, too, is often organized by natural patterns. The narrative nonfiction picture book *One Tiny Turtle* by Nicola Davies (2005) traces the life of an imaginary loggerhead turtle, telling the story of one creature, from its infancy through adulthood. Many books follow natural cycles, including *From Seed to Plant* by Gail Gibbons (2001) and *Water Is Water: A Book About the Water Cycle* by Miranda Paul (2015).

A text describing a pattern from nature generally matches the sequence of the pattern. A text about a plant or animal life cycle, for example, usually begins in infancy and ends in reproduction or death. A text about planets usually describes them in order from smallest to largest, from largest to smallest, or from their proximity to the sun. In this way, organizing writing with a natural pattern does not require much decision making about structure. If it's a rainbow, follow the colors. If it's a kitten, follow the life cycle. If it's a moon, follow the phases.

TRY IT

By observing natural structures and paying attention to patterns others ignore, students grow stronger not only as writers, but also as scientists and artists. Swanson says, "I love watching for patterns in the world and in the poetry that I read," and this life habit of watching closely has made her the kind of writer who can see a visit to Grandma's as a rainbow of things to see and taste and feel.

Go outdoors with your students. Bring clipboards. List: What do you see? What patterns do you notice? What processes are happening all around us?

Give students piles of books about nature. Ask them to study these for patterns and relationships and processes. Look back at everything you have studied in science so far this year. Together or in notebooks, make lists of processes and patterns such as

- how a shark grows teeth
- how magnetism works
- what happens in an eclipse
- how seeds travel
- what happens during migration
- how a star changes

Make time for students to write about patterns and processes they have discovered or read about. Show them how a natural pattern can help organize a piece of writing, how a writer can follow a pattern with words. Invite students to draft poems through patterns and processes, deciding

- Where will I begin?
- Where will I end?
- Will I include repetition?

Students might choose a pattern of color or number or process from the natural world and overlay it upon a different subject, as Swanson structures her visit to Grandma's through a rainbow's colors. With eyes open, young writers will uncover many new writing structures in this way.

I Am A Cloud

I am a cloud.
I sway in the wind.
I move with my family
in a great big group.
The group moves slowly.
The wind blows me.
We come together
to make rain.

by Ethan S.
Grade 1

Sunset

You pour pink and orange
on the sky,
You paint the sky
each day with your colors,
You use the same ones
every day.
You walk down behind the earth,
You wait for the moon while you walk,
You are ready to go home
since you're done.
You turn on the lights
when you go home,
You see the moon turn on his lamp,
You know your work
is over for the day

By Robbie M.
Grade 4

4

WRITERS PLAY WITH LANGUAGE

Writers make deliberate decisions about every sound and beat. If the structure or organization of a house refers to its layout, then language play is furniture selection, wall art, and color scheme. Language play is a favorite song on the radio. It is the smell of cinnamon applesauce simmering on your woodstove. It is a pillow picking up winter-blue from outside, bringing it into the living room.

Poetry offers more language play per square inch than any other genre. We hear it when we read aloud, and sometimes—as with alliteration or repetition—we even see it on the page. The sounds of wordplay are the sounds we hear in the nurseries of our apartment buildings and on the playgrounds of our schoolyards: lullabies, handclap games, jump rope rhymes, tongue twisters. Words bring humans joy, and interesting and unusual words and sound combinations enliven all genres.

When Peter Brown describes wind in *The Wild Robot* (2016)—"It bent trunks and shook branches and then—*thunk thunk thunk!*—pinecones began raining down" (20)—readers smile at his use of onomatopoeia. When Lily Shen expresses her opinion in a *New York Times Complaint Box* article, "Beware the Squirrelstein" (2011), about an overabundance of squirrels in city parks, we giggle at her simile: "While staring right at me, this brazen little creature inched closer and closer, shooting up on his hind legs between short scurries, like a furry Frankenstein." This is poetry. In prose.

Learn to Play with Language from Poems

To open the door of language play, we begin with poems. We read poems on our own, in pairs, in groups large and small. We read poems into recording devices and on stages in front of our families. We memorize poems and tap out their rhythms, counting beats and marking rhymes. We celebrate the ways that poets and poems make our mouths move, our feet tap, and our brains discover new connections.

And we talk. Talking about poetry helps us *see* and understand the language of authors who combine words in fresh and fascinating ways. When we examine poems as models of strong writing, we discuss questions including

- What interesting sounds do you hear?
- Where does the language surprise you?
- Which line makes you feel something?
- Which is your favorite line? Why?
- Which senses does the author highlight?
- Is there repetition? Where?
- Are there any comparisons in this poem?

Each writer uses the tools of wordplay differently. We call this use *voice*—the way a writer presses her fingerprint into the play dough of text. Listen to Nikki Grimes. Hear how she celebrates *word* by playing with sound, meter, verbs.

Word

Word is an
elastic thing.

Pull it, stretch it,
make it spring.

Call it music,
hear it sing.

Call it dance,
watch it swing.

Call it brick,
build a wall.

Call it snow,
see it fall.

Word is magic.
Word is all.

—*Nikki Grimes*

This chapter focuses on the "pull it, stretch it, / make it spring" playfulness of language Grimes describes, shining light on several language moves that readers appreciate in all writing. We have names for many of these—*personification, simile, onomatopoeia*. But remember, like chefs, writers are creative people, and they often invent new ways to combine phrase-ingredients and word-spices. As teachers of writing, we help students understand that poets play with language in the same ways that information, opinion, and story writers do. Strong writing is strong writing regardless of genre, and our work is to help students pack suitcases full of metaphor and imagery, inviting them to open these suitcases whenever they write.

Morning Dog

In the morning
I shake my new collar sharply
and look up to see if the mound moves.

If it has,
if it has not,
either way

I wander to the bedside
sniff, sniff, sniff
working my nose under the blanket.

Asking.

If she lifts the blanket
I'm good.
It's morning.

Otherwise
it must not be
and I wander back to my post and lie down.

If she lifts the blanket
she'll also open her mouth at me
breathing out.

Oh,
what a good and glorious gift!
Morning breath.

—*April Halprin Wayland*

WORDS FROM THE POET

I look for ways to make my thoughts look poem-ish. *Move your words around like puzzle pieces. You won't know what works until—click!—they snap into place. Mess around: break your words into couplets (two lines) or quatrains (four lines). In this poem, triplets looked best and the words made sense when I broke them up in groups of three. I use line breaks instead of commas. I'm telling the reader where to breathe. (PS: I didn't write this poem. My dog Eli did.)*

CONSIDER THE TECHNIQUE

Line breaks are perhaps the most distinctive feature of poetry. You can usually tell if a text is a poem just from how it looks. As April Halprin Wayland explains, line breaks tell "the reader where to breathe." Line breaks offer a visual space around words that tells us to linger and keeps us from hurrying.

Line breaks in poetry are much like phrasing in prose. When we teach our students to write compound and complex sentences, we teach them about clauses and phrases. We teach them to briefly pause at appropriate punctuation, and we model this by reading aloud. Wayland's words, "I use line breaks instead of commas," will help students understand this connection.

A writer may break a line in order to

- indicate a pause, much like a comma

- highlight a repeating line, usually formatting it the same way each time

- allow one word to stand alone, spotlighting its importance

- break up a very long phrase, so that its length does not distract

- create a sound pattern

- create a visual pattern

- break a pattern, reflecting a meaning change

Notice how Wayland's poem is broken up into three-line stanzas, except for that one-word line, "Asking." Anyone who knows dogs knows this moment. Asking. By setting one word apart, Wayland makes her readers to pause and wait, just as the dog-speaker must wait to find out if it is morning—or not. Writers of information and opinion and story do this too. The one-word sentence stops a reader, makes him pay attention.

In the same way that poets decide how to lay out text, writers of other genres also choose to set off text in various ways and sometimes to play with font and text size. Students can learn from what they notice visually in texts, and we can encourage them to notice the following in any genre:

- punctuation

- text layout

- print variation

- font changes

- space created by ellipses, dashes, indentations, or simply white space

TRY IT

To help students hear the sound of line breaks, read poems aloud. Be sure to read poetry with attention to meaning, and do not simply stop woodenly at the end of each line. Choose one poem, perhaps "Morning Dog," and read it several times. Allow students to hear the wee-breath pauses between lines, and ask them to listen for meaning. Make time for partners to read poems aloud with each other, discussing which reading sounds best and why. They may even choose to mark parts of a poem to guide their reading: where to pause, which words to accent, where to slow down or speed up. What do they notice about the line breaks?

I recall experimenting with line breaks once with my fifth graders. I removed line breaks from Edna St. Vincent Millay's "Lament" (1981) and gave each student a copy of the poem written-as-paragraph. Each student reshaped the words into poems, and we shared how we made line break decisions.

Many of your students will write poems that sound like poems but look like paragraphs. Simply say, "Your poem sounds like a poem, but it looks like a paragraph. Let me help you with the line breaks." Then ask the student to read the poem slowly, listening for natural pauses and looking for punctuation that might suggest line breaks. Demonstrate how to make slash marks to show where the line breaks will go when the poem is recopied.

Another neat exercise, shared with me by a teacher friend, is to write each line of a poem on a sentence strip or an index card and then move these lines into different possible arrangements, much like magnetic poetry. As Wayland advises, "Move your words around like puzzle pieces. You won't know what works until—*click!*—they snap into place."

Ask your students to choose paragraphs from their writers' notebooks or from other texts and to reshape these as poems by adding line breaks. This is called "found poetry" and it's a neat way to open your eyes to the poems all around.

Once students have experience reading poems aloud and thinking about how line breaks affect the look and sound of poetry, bring this same sensibility to prose. Remember that in many ways, as Wayland explains, punctuation is the line break of prose. Ask students to read paragraphs they are drafting aloud to see where their voices naturally pause. Is there a mark of punctuation here? Should there be? Teach students to ask, "Could I lay this out differently for a different impact?"

One of the most important lessons you will teach your students related to line breaks and phrasing is the value of reading their writing aloud. Say, "As authors, you drive the writing bus. You determine when your readers keep going and when they pause and stop to look around."

STUDENT POEMS TO SHARE

Rain is a lullabye

Rain takes me to places
Alaska
chicago
and even acient Greece
I see the images of places
I want to go
like a magic mirror
inside these little rain drops
rain is a lullabye
calling to me

by Mo M., Grade 3

Sadness

I was sitting in my bed
Looking at my Closets
When I heard
Stomping
up the stairs
I Looked outside my door
I ran to my parents room
I saw my brother
Crying
And then I
Ran
Down
The stairs
I went into the living room
And I saw my parrakeet
Dead
Then I went
Down on my knees
And started crying too
By: Catalina B.
Grade 3

Nest

Hidden on the top
of the green shade,
nest of twigs
and shadows,
smaller than any
of my fingers,
lingers the tiny nest.
Best I not open
the window,
or let the shade down,
or that smudge,
nudged by a breeze,
will be squeezed out of
sanctuary.
Egg-laden, unwary,
it will slide down
onto the deck,
unheard:
a wreckage
of unborn birds.

—*Jane Yolen*

WORDS FROM THE POET

To find surprising words like smudged, sanctuary, wreckage, *I used to spend time perusing (another great word!) the thesaurus and dictionaries, because poets need to know a variety of words. Now I mostly* rummage *(another good one!) through my mind. The French poet-philosopher Paul Valéry used to say that a poem is never finished but is only abandoned. I prefer saying that the words in a poem are never finished until you find the exact right one.*

For me the "right" word has to paint a picture, sing a song, and have at least one perfect meaning. (Extra points if it has two or more.) For me smudge *is that word. At first I wrote* nest *partially because it was a placeholder and partially because I liked the way* nest *and* nudged *both started with an* n. *But after a few revisions, I realized I didn't want to repeat the word* nest. *So then I tried other, similar words. I finally settled on* smudge—*which can mean either something in art, or a bit of sooty-ness, or something damaged. And it also has another meaning—something small and insignificant. Also, it rhymed with* nudge. *Win-win! See how I did that?*

Consider the Technique

Listeners are unmoved by cliché. Readers are bored by buzzwords. In all times and professions—including teaching and writing—certain phrases become too-well-worn-to-inspire. (Think *differentiation*.) When these words pop up in meetings, our eyes cloud, and we zone into mental catnaps. Writers must not offer stale bread to hungry readers.

One of the gifts of reading lies in the flavor that someone else's language adds to our own experiences or perceptions. When we read an unusual (but not too unusual) description of an object or feeling or action, we suddenly understand a piece of the world differently. Striving to change readers through words, writers must care about each word they write.

In her *Ask* article "Nosy News" (2016), Elizabeth Preston describes chameleon tongues: "When a chameleon sees a tasty bug, it shoots out its tongue, and—thwap!—the bug is lunch" (2). In Andrea Davis Pinkney's *Ella Fitzgerald: The Tale of a Vocal Virtuosa* (2002), narrator Scat Cat Monroe describes Fitzgerald's early voice: "At first, her voice came quiet as a whisper. A measly little hiss, soft as a cricket. But when the band joined in, Ella rolled out a tune sweet enough to bake." Such combinations of words delight us, for likely we have never seen or heard them together before.

When choosing words, writers think about how readers will respond, fine-tuning phrases to perk up readers' ears. Writers ask themselves questions about the words they choose, including

- Have I written any clichés?

- Can I strengthen any nouns through specificity? Not *dog*, for example, but *beagle*.

- Where can I make a verb do more work? Not *said loudly*, for example, but *shouted*.

- Can I replace any stale or repeated words?

By learning to appreciate the thoughtful word choices authors make, students will become more thoughtful about their own written words.

TRY IT

As Jane Yolen explains, she once spent time perusing thesauruses and dictionaries, filling her mind with rich, interesting words. Encourage your students to do the same, to wallow in the sounds of words and grow their own word gardens, listing favorites in their notebooks. I keep a list of my own favorite words in the back of each of my notebooks. These words find their way into my essays and stories, during the time I am keeping that notebook—and beyond.

Delve into books with students, searching for unusual descriptions or word combinations. Invite students to collect these "Words We Adore" or "Striking Phrases" or "Poetry in Prose" on a bulletin board or in a class notebook.

Students might translate fresh language they find back into stale language, perhaps on a T-chart: "Fresh Language / Stale Language." This "turning strong into weak" exercise can make cliché clear to students who may not initially recognize the tired words in their own writing.

Include "revise for cliché" as a regular habit, requiring students to reread their work, crossing out and reworking phrases they know they have heard before. Highlight student revisions that upgrade stale combinations of word and phrase. Talk about places where students notice that their own writing has been deepened by one specific change of word or phrase.

Writing becomes more poetic, persuasive, and powerful as students learn to seek beyond the first word that comes to mind. Like Yolen, they too can work to "find the exact right one."

The Moon Is Me

I swim gracefully in the sky,
Breathing my giant cool breaths,
I have a few freckles, but,
don't judge me,
Not even a little bit,
Grin as you sleep,
Dream your best dreams,
Chase your dreams fast,
While,
I lull you to sleep,
Shh,
Goodnight!

By Nora P.
Grade 3

Summer on Lillis Road

The forenoon sun crawling into the open window
Morning dew seeping between my exposed toes
Gravel crunching under the wheels of my bike
Soft voices conversing in the early light

Prickers scratching my tanned skin
The slapping of sticks and leaves, into my face
More waiting for open air, and open space

Legs pumping through the morning mist
Awakening crickets singing
Dogs barking as we pedal past the concealing palisade

Gardeners laughing while gardening the elysian estate
More glee, more pedaling
Time to turn around just in time for breakfast

by Jessica W.
Grade 8

Mary Todd Lincoln Speaks
of Her Son's Death, 1862

When Willie died of the fever
Abraham spoke the words
that I could not:
"My boy is gone.
He is actually gone."

Gone.
The word was a thunder clap
deafening me to my wails
as I folded over his body
already growing cold.

Gone.
The word was a curtain
coming down on 11 years,
hiding toy soldiers,
circus animals,
and his beloved train.

Gone.
The word was poison
but poison that would not kill
only gag me with its bitterness
as I choked on a prayer for my death.

Abraham spoke the words
that I could not:
"My boy is gone.
He is actually gone."
And I am left
with grief
when spoken
shatters like my heart.

—*Paul B. Janeczko*

WORDS FROM THE POET

Repetition can be soothing, like the waves on the beach or the breathing of a child in your arms. But it can also be a reminder, and that's what I was trying to do by repeating the word gone *in my poem. It is a one-syllable reminder—"a thunderclap"—to the characters and to the reader of the enormous finality of Willie's death. I wanted that word to echo with my readers, the way it echoes in the broken hearts of the boy's parents.*

CONSIDER THE TECHNIQUE

We know repetition in the world of fashion and interior design: a young man's peach bow tie matches his date's prom dress, my seafoam towels match my outdated bathroom tile. Repetition "ties it all together."

Writers use repetition in various ways. A writer may repeat an image, a symbol, a line, a word. As Paul B. Janeczko explains, "Repetition can be soothing, like the waves on the beach or the breathing of a child in your arms. But it can also be a reminder." Repetition underlines an important point, and repeated lines sear themselves into readers' minds.

More than fifty years after Dr. Martin Luther King Jr. delivered his "I Have a Dream" speech (1963), we remember it today for the strength of his words and also for the power of those four repeated words. King repeats "I have a dream" eight times, closely followed by "Let freedom ring," which he repeats seven times. With each repetition, the words sink in more deeply.

Repetition may hold parts of a text together or may drive the structure of a whole piece. In the songs of childhood and in popular music, a repeated chorus invites us to join in and captures the essence of the song. Writers of prose sometimes use repetition in a similar way. For example, in the picture book *Newspaper Hats* (2016) by Phil Cummings, a child wants his grandfather to remember who he is. Cummings highlights the grandfather's memory loss by having the child repeat, "Do you remember me?" much like a chorus, throughout the first half of the story.

A writer may also use repetition in a series of sentences. In the picture book *Stepping Stones: A Refugee Family's Journey* (2016), Margriet Ruurs weaves repetition into a description of memories: "In that not-so-distant memory we were free. Free to play, free to go to school. Free to buy fruit and vegetables at the market. Free to laugh and chat, drink tea with neighbors. Always three cups."

Chapter books often rely on repetition of details and images to help readers keep their bearings. An "I've heard this before" feeling deepens the experience of a text. Regardless of how or why it is used, readers enjoy repetition. Readers enjoy repetition.

TRY IT

First, talk with students about repetition in the world outside of texts—socks matching team shirts, flowers matching a front door. Ask, "What do you see that repeats?" Look around the classroom—find math patterns with blocks, repeated designs in artwork. Tell students that writers repeat too. Writers repeat words and phrases to emphasize important ideas and to tie parts of texts together.

Read some favorite texts together in any genre and look for different types of repetition—words, phrases, sounds, or ideas. Older students might do this independently or in small groups, underlining the repetition they find. Discuss the effect of the repetition and how it adds to the readers' interpretation and experience with these texts. Develop some language that helps students name how to use repetition in their own writing, chart it, and invite young writers to imitate an author's use of repetition.

You might model revising a draft by layering in repetition, weaving a meaningful phrase through your own writing. Show students how you experiment with repetition one way, then another. In and out, like sewing small stitches, repetition can bring many scattered words into patterns of significance.

The Kittens

Once I found a kitten
The kitten was gray
Gray like the clouds
On a rainy day
Once I found a kitten
The kitten was brown
Brown like the dirt
In the center of town
Once I found a kitten
The kitten was black
Black like the coal
At the bottom of a sack
Once I found a kitten
The kitten was white
White like the moon
On the blanket of night.
— Bobby, 4th Grade

The Darkness

Down
under the waves
under the light
into the dark

Down
Spakling eyes
under the waves
glittering swimmers

Under the waves

Down

Down into darkness
the light
slowly fading

Gone
under the dark
under the light
under the waves
Beaneath the sea...

Ian G.
grade 4

Pelican

The sea is
a blue window
tinted with golden rays.
Quiet as a dream
you fold your wings
and tumble
through glass,
your orange beak
bulging with
silver shards.

—*Joyce Sidman*

In this poem, I wanted to capture the feeling of early morning on the beach watching pelicans dive. The ocean has many moods, but on that day it was absolutely still and serene—like a blue window. Using metaphor like this allows you to add mood or emotion to your writing.

CONSIDER THE TECHNIQUE

When we northerners say, "The world is covered in a blanket of snow," we know we are not looking at a bed blanket. When we hear America described as a "tossed salad," we realize that our people come from many lands and live together. Metaphors frame the world in surprising ways, deepening our understandings, placing vivid images in readers' minds.

Skillfully wrought, metaphors create newness, forever changing the way a reader sees something. In her poem "In the Nursing Home" (1997), Jane Kenyon describes an old woman as a horse in a pasture that gets smaller and smaller, waiting for the day that her Master will lead her home. I first read Kenyon's poem when my own grandmother lived in a nursing home, after having lived in an apartment and before that, in her big house. Seeing Grandma's life-space shrink as a horse's pasture might shrink lit a spark in my reading heart. "Yes," I thought, "it's *just* like that." This realization made me feel sad, and it also made me feel understood, as if Kenyon had read my heart. Writers lead readers to such flashes of "Yes!" by describing things as other things through metaphor.

Many metaphors ("blanket of snow," "tossed salad") have become cliché, and these are not the metaphors we strive to write. Rather, writers work to make new metaphors that lead readers from one topic to another in a way that may first seem unusual, but comes to feel perfectly right. A strong metaphor helps us understand something in a brand-new way, and thanks to Joyce Sidman's "Pelican," when I now see a real pelican, I will imagine water as "a blue window," will see fish as "silver shards." When a writer—in any genre—offers this newness, a reader's view of the world is changed as one thing so briefly becomes another.

In her memoir *The Sound of a Wild Snail Eating* (2010), Elisabeth Tova Bailey recounts memories of the small snail she observed as she recovered from illness. Describing how its quiet ways calmed her frazzled mind, she writes, "With its mysterious, fluid movement, the snail was the quintessential tai chi master" (26). For a reader who knows tai chi, this metaphor makes clear Bailey's relationship to her snail, thus changing forever how one sees snails.

In their *National Geographic* article "The Caribbean's Crown Jewels" (2016), authors and photographers David Doubilet and Jennifer Hayes describe sharks as forming "a perfect carousel around us" (101) and marine worms as creating "a living veil" (103). These metaphors help readers experience Caribbean creatures in terms they know from their landlubber lives.

Writers in all genres rely on metaphor, holding readers' hands as they leap from across the creek, from the stone of reality to the stone of imagination. As Sidman says, "Using metaphor . . . allows you to add mood." And as they add mood, metaphors transform one thing to another, just for an eyeblink—and maybe forever.

TRY IT

Collect examples of brilliant metaphors you find in texts of all genres. The best way for students to become adept at using any writing technique is to find and study many examples, so create "Favorite Metaphor" lists in notebooks or on a bulletin board, sharing what makes each one effective.

On the flip side, collect clichéd comparisons, discussing how to go beyond them. Every cliché was once fresh, but like bags of lettuce in the fridge, freshness doesn't last long. I often Google my metaphors, asking, "Did I think of this, or have I read this forty-seven times before?" Experienced writers sport invisible bumper stickers: "I revise for cliché."

Introduce metaphor by playing a pass-the-object game with students, one I learned from a teacher friend long ago. Sit in a circle, and slowly pass an object such as a dried flower (natural objects are inherently inspiring) around the room. As each child holds the object, listen as she renames it: "It's a magic wand," "It's a letter *I*," "It's a raccoon spine," "It's a chopstick. . . ."

Start by looking at one object from your backpack or from a class box of inspiration-objects, or go outside to list things you see. Now, using metaphor, turn one of your objects into something different:

- This ladybug is a grandma wearing a polka-dot coat.

- My scarf is a swirling blue river.

- Shells on the beach are teeth the ocean lost.

- A zebra is a maze with legs.

Once you have admired and discussed metaphors that make you see the world anew, encourage your students to regularly look for metaphors in their reading and to intentionally build metaphors, kneading them naturally into all their writing: fiction, personal narrative, information, opinion, and poetry.

A Tree is a broom,
with along handle
for the ground To hold
its leaves sweep away the
brushing away clouds
and blotting out the sun.

by Maggie B
grade 3

Petals Are Sky Divers

Petals are sky divers,
jumping off the tree.

floating,
hovering,
down to the ground.

A waterfall,
of white petals.

Petals are
sky divers.

by Cole
grade 3

a dream is like

a dream is like
a house with se
cret rooms and mir
rored halls a dream
is like a chi
nese vase you catch
before it falls
a dream is like
a talking fish
that fascinates
the net a dream
is like a let
ter from a you
you haven't met

—*David Elliott*

WORDS FROM THE POET

I try not to settle for the first comparison that comes to mind since it's often the most obvious, and therefore the least interesting. The best similes should surprise both the reader and the writer. And don't be afraid to help your simile out by adding an adjective or an adjective clause. There's a difference between a dream is like a vase *and* a dream is like a Chinese vase you catch before it falls.

CONSIDER THE TECHNIQUE

In the same way that all kittens are cats but all cats are not kittens, all similes are metaphors but all metaphors are not similes. A simile is a comparison that uses *like* or *as* to draw two things together; we do not say or imply that one *is* the other, just that it is *like* or *as* the other. David Elliott's "a dream is like / a house with se / cret rooms and mir / rored halls" offers a connection between dream and house, allowing us to nod, "Why yes, indeed. A dream *is* like that." Yet he does not go so far as to say, "A dream *is* a house. . . ." I once read that similes are more tentative than metaphors. With a simile, a writer draws a line between two things, showing how they are similar. With a metaphor, a writer turns one thing into another for a moment. A simile feels like a comparison. A metaphor, like enchantment.

A well-chosen simile is not likely to have been heard or read before. It's not as green as grass or as fresh as a daisy. It's new, but not as new as freshly fallen snow. Rather, it's as new as a puppy's first romp in that same snow. Elliott explains, "I try not to settle for the first comparison that comes to mind since it's often the most obvious, and therefore the least interesting." Again, avoid cliché. Not like the plague, necessarily, but like a bad old boyfriend.

Herein lies an important piece of writing advice of which writers often speak, but that students rarely hear. In Elliott's words, strong writing "should surprise both the reader *and* the writer." Such advice can be frustrating for linear types, but we cannot dismiss it. There is a twinkle of mystery in writing, and when students understand that a word or simile or connection may occasionally arrive unbidden, they will remain open to this possibility.

We find similes in all genres of writing as people love making connections. For example, in his informational book *Sharks* (1995), Seymour Simon writes, "Sharks are *like* 'swimming noses,' and can detect even tiny amounts of blood in the water." Look for similes in fiction, in scientific descriptions, in historical references, and in opinion pieces.

TRY IT

As with metaphors, have students collect similes in their notebooks. Teach them to stand back, take a deep breath, and say, "Whoa. That's some simile." Remember that when you model this gasp, students understand that such a simile-gasp is possible. Compare similes and metaphors. What do your students notice?

Many teachers and authors suggest listing emotions and feelings, such as joyful, sad, embarrassed, or angry. Ask students to choose a feeling, tying it to an object from the world with the words *like* or *as*:

- She felt lonely, like an old bike.

- He was as lonely as a new kid.

You might try this exercise outdoors, observing trees and bugs, flowers and sky, comparing natural objects to other objects. The Private Eye curriculum (see page 30), through the use of jewelers' loupes, teaches writers to do this through close observation and sketching, using visual observations to draw comparisons.

Taking Elliott's advice, invite your students to add more to their similes by adding an adjective or an adjective clause:

- She felt lonely, like an old bike out for the trash.

- He was as lonely as a new kid eating lunch with the nurse.

Look at photographs and works of art, or scenes in the classroom, making similes using the five senses:

- It looked like/as . . .

- It smelled like/as . . .

- It sounded like/as . . .

- It felt like/as . . .

- It tasted like/as . . .

- It is like/as . . .

Notebook play offers students opportunities to try out new language moves, or it may serve as revision work as students dance back into drafts, choosing lines to elevate with comparison. A student may build a new piece of writing from a list of similes as Elliott does here, or from just one comparison, weaving it throughout a story, description, opinion piece, or other text.

life

As gentle as eyes
As smooth as water
A form of life
A baby is born.

by Corbin D.
Grade 3

LEAVES

Leaves are like
musical notes
falling into order
to make a song

BY Grady M.
Grade 3

Suspense

Wide-eyed
the sunflowers
stare and catch their summer
breath, while I pause, holding basket
and shears.

—*Deborah Chandra*

© 2018 by Amy Ludwig VanDerwater, from *Poems Are Teachers*. Portsmouth, NH: Heinemann.

WORDS FROM THE POET

Some people believe the entire world is made of consciousness—there is plant consciousness, animal consciousness, even earth consciousness. Seeing things from a human perspective helps us feel their secret life force.

In the poem "Suspense," the sunflowers become like us—holding their breath. And in that moment we are inseparable, for our eyes too can grow wide with fear. As we give human traits to things, they return to us a quality of ourselves hidden in them.

If we behold a flower, a mountain, a mouse as a "Thou" instead of an "it," we can hear them speak. Not with words. But in their own peculiar language they whisper, chatter, and hint of a boundless vitality and deeper unity we all share.

My second-grade students loved show-and-tell and shared the things they brought to school as if they held a touch of majesty or a living presence. Bryan held up his lost tooth as if it glowed like a rising moon. Ireyna saw her pet tarantula as a fragile beauty named Crystal. As Ireyna spoke, we forgot the spider's strangeness and saw that in everything there is more than we realize. When familiar facts take on a magical freshness, when the mundane gives way to the miraculous—this is poetry.

CONSIDER THE TECHNIQUE

Truth be told, I cannot choose a favorite color because I am afraid of hurting all the other colors' feelings. To me, the world is alive, and every inanimate object feels alive too. I first read "Suspense" in 1994, and when it was time to choose a model of personification for this book, Deborah Chandra's spare text immediately rose to mind. "Sunflowers / stare and catch their summer / breath"—never, but of course!

When we personify an animal or an object, we give it human qualities. Tomatoes blush and cats sit on our keyboards not because it is summer and keyboards are warm, but because tomatoes are embarrassed and cats have novels to write. Our broken dishwasher is angry at us, and we ask our stalling cars, "What did I do to you?"

Writers, too, personify animals and objects because personification makes something not-like-us feel like-us. And when we feel close to something, we are less likely to alienate it and more likely to care about it. Personification quickly makes a subject relatable—even if it is but a broken shell. After all, that broken shell has secrets, just like you or me. This something may be an inanimate object, such as a pencil or bus; it may be something living like a plant, or it may be something even more human-like, such as a dog. Most people with pets regularly give them human qualities, but giving human qualities to a bicycle is even more surprising and quirky. In Cynthia Rylant's picture book *The Old Woman Who Named Things*, the main character has outlived all her friends and so names inanimate objects. Car, chair, house: these are her friends.

In her narrative nonfiction picture book *Bat Loves the Night* (2004), Nicola Davies describes Bat not as "the bat" but as "Bat" with a capital *B*. *Bat* is her name. She writes, "In the east, the sky is getting light. It is past Bat's bedtime." Suddenly, this animal we feared just yesterday is adorable, with a name and a snuggly bedtime. Similarly, in Dianna Hutts Aston's series of picture books including *A Seed Is Sleepy* and *A Rock Is Lively*, Aston lists many personified traits of natural objects, following them up with scientific facts.

As Chandra explains, when we listen with our careful ears to the mysterious messages we take from the objects and animals we write about, we may learn not only about them, but about ourselves too. And through our writing, our readers become more connected to the animals and objects of the world.

TRY IT

If you have not made show-and-tell a part of your classroom community, do so now. You might call it something different, but as Chandra describes, offering students time to talk about the things they hold dear will open doorways for connecting conversations. Pass a treasured object and talk. What might it think? When students open their consciousness to the possibility of a rock thinking or a watch remembering a grandfather, it helps them see the world anew, a valuable skill for writers of all genres.

Writers can personify animals or inanimate objects by using concrete words: nouns, adjectives, and verbs. Just think about my old blue hatchback. If I want to personify my trusty 2011 Pontiac Vibe, I might do so as follows:

- Nouns: stomach (gas tank), eyes (headlights), bedroom (garage)

- Verbs: sleeping, hurrying, complaining

- Adjectives: tired, grumpy, excited, sick, proud

Invite students to play with personification by choosing an inanimate object (you might set up a table of objects) or animal. Ask them to list in their notebooks specific nouns, verbs, and adjectives to give this object or animal human qualities. Where might this lead an information writer, an opinion writer, a story writer? These lists may remain as pages of notebook play, or students may develop them into publishable texts, about the sadness of our warming earth perhaps, or the way certain books sing your name.

If your students are drafting, invite them to dive back in and see if there are places where objects or animals might be described with human traits or emotions. As with any technique, students' early attempts at personification may feel awkward, but as Katie Wood Ray teaches us in *Study Driven* (2006), what students learn through revision first, they bring later to their first drafts (30).

Small Boulder

Winter, Spring, Summer, and fall - all the
Seasons. it is always there. Never breaks,
Never moves. All around the world, from atlahtic
to Pacific you can see them.
On the earth for millions of years
and will stay there for a million more.
Brown, black, gray, white with cuts and bumps.
Looks at you with his worn-out eyes and mouth.

Sees all, sees you, sees the kids at school.
They build and knock him down.
Step on him.

He wishes he was a boulder instead of a
Pebble.
And then he remembers all the wonderful
things at the school.
He can see the children laugh and play.
and All the seasons Winter, Spring Summer
and fall.
He fills up with enjoyment.

by Shealynn C.   Grade 2

Beanbag
Colors
comfort
squishy and warm,
But now there are holes,
and no one can sit.
The books are gone,
but it lies in the attic,
wondering where the books are?
And crying for company.

by Lisa S
grade 5

Go Away, Cat

Leave me alone,
you cyclone of
fur and whiskers.
Stop nuzzling my arm.
Stop purring
your low thunder rumble.
I can't pet you now.

I'll not leave you alone.
I'll not stop my storming.
Pet me now,
or be warned—
this dark cloud
claws sharp streaks
of lightning.

—*Ann Whitford Paul*

WORDS FROM THE POET

Most of us are lazy and let our eyes do the describing. Work to strengthen your senses beyond sight. Close your eyes and hear the robin outside singing. Touch your lumpy chair fabric. Smell the soapy clean of your shirt. Taste and savor the sweetness of your candy. Describing with more than one sense invites your reader to more easily enter your scene.

CONSIDER THE TECHNIQUE

Ann Whitford Paul's advice to "close your eyes" in order to strengthen your senses is wise, especially for humans who spend hours daily interacting visually with screens. Paying attention to each sense takes practice, and making time for this practice is time well spent; it is what writers do. Writers need sharp senses, to create worlds-out-of-senses on flat paper pages.

Writers of all genres know that readers are drawn into writing through their senses. Much of what we read requires that we imagine places or historical time periods we have never seen, realities we have never imagined. We come to understand these different worlds through our bodies, through our senses of sight, smell, hearing, taste, and touch. Writers make readers feel what is not there, hear who is not speaking, smell smells built from alphabet letters and spaces and ink.

When we read Paul's "Go Away, Cat," we see and feel the cat in the room with us, but not because Paul writes, "I see . . . , I feel. . . ." Rather, she hints at the various ways this cat makes itself known. "Cyclone of fur and whiskers" offers our eyes fuzz and movement. "Nuzzling" offers our fingers the feel of a kitty's head. "Purring" and "low thunder" offer our ears the sound of cat.

In the Newbery Honor–winning *Bomb: The Race to Build—and Steal— the World's Most Dangerous Weapon* (2012), Steve Sheinkin describes the moment that Harry Gold knew that FBI agents were onto him: "Gold watched Brennan slide a thick, tattered copy of Principals of Chemical Engineering from the shelf. Nausea swelled Gold's throat as he saw a brown, folded street map drop to the floor. To Gold, the map seemed to scream its title in the silent room" (2). In this short sensory passage, we see, feel, and hear.

In her novel *The Fourteenth Goldfish* (2014), Jennifer L. Holm describes a dance through Ellie's eyes: "The music pounds like a pulse through the floor, and it's so loud, you can't think. It feels like the undertow of the ocean, and I'm just swept along, everything reduced to senses. The sticky heat of the air. The brush of an elbow. The flash of a strobe light" (130). The feel of the music, the feel of heat and elbow, the flash of light—we are in this place.

Writers are sensitive, and a writer's selection of sensory details touches parts of a reader's brain, for through our bodies, we make sense of the world, in texts as well as in 3-D.

TRY IT

In order to get in touch (or in sight, smell, hearing, or taste) with our senses, we must, as Paul reminds us, work at it. Some of this work might be in the form of writing exercises. Take your students out of the classroom, to a courtyard or art room or library. Bring notebooks and jot. Say, "What do you hear? What do you smell? Remember to close your eyes as this will help you focus on one sense at a time."

Bring objects into the classroom. Explore them with your senses. What does cinnamon smell like? What does a stuffed teddy bear feel like? Practice describing experiences with your senses without using the words *see, taste, touch, feel,* or *hear*—just as Paul helps us feel cat scratches as "streaks of lightning" without ever using the word *touch* or *feel*.

If your students are working on drafts in other genres, ask them to enhance parts of these drafts with sensory description. Model this with your own writing, selecting a setting, object, person, or animal you wish bring to life with senses. Write this topic atop a new notebook page, and below it list the senses: sight, hearing, smell, touch, taste. From these lists, add sensory description.

If students revise for sensory language, consider sharing before and after versions of drafts, discussing how such revisions lift the work. If you keep a class writing scrapbook, save a few pages for recording sensory-rich passages from students' independent reading and from content-area reading. Keep the senses alive, cycling back to this exploration in every unit of writing you teach. How do information writers appeal to readers' senses? Opinion writers?

Rock Man

The Rock is wearing wan out Clothes.
They smell old.
It has a gray face,
as bumpy as the roof of your mouth.
my roock is knocking on the door.

by Dylan K.
grade 4

Winter

Tree Branches
Are covered i
In white.

The ground
Crunches
Under your heavy boots.

Small dots of white
gently coat
your face.

by Jeffrey Z.
grade 6

Roam Poem

A rhyming ram named Roman
Roamed and roamed and roamed.
One day he rhymed and roamed to Rome.
He roamed atop a Roman dome
Then rhyming Roman roamed back home
And wrote this roaming rhyming poem.

—*Douglas Florian*

WORDS FROM THE POET

A friend of mine, author Dan Gutman, stopped by my studio yesterday. When he mentioned that he had recently traveled to Rome, I started to picture him roaming around Rome. Those two words, Rome *and* roam, *sound the same but have different meanings. That's called a* homophone *and it can be the start of a poem. I searched for other words with a similar sound and came up with* ram *and* rhyme *and the name* Roman. *Then I created a little story poem using rhyme. The tricky part was getting this roaming ram to rhyme. Using homophones and puns in a poem is called* wordplay *and I love to employ wordplay.*

CONSIDER THE TECHNIQUE

In the same way a child will giggle through a bath, repeating "Bubble! Bubble! Bubble!" writers take pleasure in the sounds of words, in combining, inventing, and juggling words in new ways. Writers regularly change and invent new words, and as Douglas Florian fiddled with the words *Rome* and *roam* in his mind, he invented a new story too. Wordplay gave him a new writing idea.

Usually, writers rely on real words one can look up in a dictionary, but sometimes writers invent new words. On his website, Andrew Clements describes how he came upon the idea for his novel *Frindle*. During a talk to students, Clements explained that words are all invented by people "and that new words get made up all the time" (2014). This led him to wordplay, which led him to *Frindle*.

Many authors play with word sounds. Think of Dr. Seuss and those truffula trees. Or a writer may smush two words together to make a brand-new word. Florian does this often in poems, even in the title of his autumn poetry book, *Autumnblings*, a combination of *autumn* and *tumbling*, and his summer poetry book, *Summersaults*, a new spelling of this word to reflect the season.

A writer may spell a word unconventionally, to emphasize how he wants readers to read the word. In Sarah E. Coleman's article "Get Over It!" (2017) in *Young Rider* magazine, she stretches out a word for meaning: "If you don't seriously lock on and stare down the line of jumps, dead in the center, your steed will slowwwlllly start drifting to one side of the fence or another" (26).

A writer may thread words together with dashes, thus creating a super-long word with a new meaning, as Bob Graham does in describing "chew-it-up-and-spit-it-out-at-you dogs" in *"Let's Get a Pup!" Said Kate* (2001). A writer can play with the sounds of homophones and rhymes that sound interesting together, as Florian does in "Roam Poem."

When writers play with words, they're thinking not about rules but about exploration, meaning, and sound. Literary playfulness enlivens a reader's experience. When writers use familiar words in new ways, they wake their readers up. *Frindle* does not mean "pen," but oh, it could. May we all read aloud and then pause, smiling at arrangements of letters and sounds we have never before encountered. And then may we hand our students frindles so they can play too.

TRY IT

Again, you can invite students to pay close attention to the meanings and sounds of words by encouraging them to become word keepers, to find joy in the sounds of language, to choose favorite words as one chooses favorite smooth stones at the creek's edge. In the same way that Donovan in *Donovan's Word Jar* by Monalisa DeGross collects words in a jar, your students can collect words on special pages of their notebooks or on a class bulletin board. This list, from one of my own notebooks, inspired the poem "Word Collection" in my poetry book *Read! Read! Read!*

Word List from Amy's Notebook

Making word lists has taught me that I adore the short *i* sound. I only know this because these words appear on my lists repeatedly: *mitten, wink, wish, quilt, serendipity, whisper, winter.* I enjoy knowing that I have a favorite sound, and young writers enjoy learning about their favorite words and sounds too.

Make time for your students to play with these word lists, pairing or combining groups or words in various ways. From my list above, I might combine two words into one, forming the new word *winterwish*. Encourage students to write from their new combinations, discovering the new ideas that emerge from wordplay.

Ask students to share invented words of their own or words invented by family or friends. Our son invented the word *fooping*, a combination of *fake* and *pooping*, to name his habit of reading in the bathroom when I call him to the kitchen for dishes. This bit of wordplay on his part could inspire an essay on mine.

Like Florian, your students might fiddle with homophones, making pairs such as *fir/fur* or *prince/prints*, and then choosing one pair for writing inspiration. Experiment with writing from pairings that tickle you, as Florian did with "Roam Poem."

Stop and talk when your students encounter nifty wordplay or invention in texts, admiring the ways writers mix, create, and juggle language to surprise and delight.

STUDENT POEMS TO SHARE

The Tool That Came To School

I'm Scared
My heart is bruised with Panic
My state of mind is frantic
This Pocket Knife found it's way to my backPack
Now that I look back I left it in there from Germany
The tool came to School accidentally
But the teacher is Still Scolding me
oh what a fool I am as I Sit on this Stool
AS the knife is brought to the Principal
I know my moral Principles I told you it was an accident
It won't happen again
Here I Sit on this Stool I'm frowning now I'm drowning now
In my own fears in my own tears oh dear!

by Jeremy P.
Grade 8

"River Song"

Rushing water
Bubbling-Splashing
Wind whistling
Leaves dancing

Birds chirping
Fluttering-flying
Grass swaying
Trees waving

Rustling leaves
Tumbling-Rocks
Earth will only dance
To Nature's music box.

by: Charlotte P.
Grade 6

Rhythm

Rain Song

Rain taps out a rhythm,
a rapid skipping rhythm
a plitter-plinking, plopping,
hopping, bopping kind of beat.

It starts with just a drizzle
a syncopated sizzle,
a sound that soon becomes a tune
as raindrops hit the street.

It sets my toes to tapping,
I'm twirling and I'm clapping,
Splashing, dashing, laughing
as I move my dancing feet.

Play the water music,
the thrilling, trilling music!
Spill the notes from every cloud,
DripDrop, PlipPlop. Repeat!

—*Kristy Dempsey*

WORDS FROM THE POET

It's hard for me to imagine writing without rhythm, without the ability to use the sounds words make, as well as the way I phrase them, to inform both the meaning and the mood I want my words to create. To me, all writing is made to be read out loud, to be heard and even performed! *When I'm writing, both poetry and prose, you'll find me tapping my hands or feet, dancing and jumping, and using my mouth and tongue to make sounds—almost like beatboxing—so I can listen to the rhythm of my words.*

CONSIDER THE TECHNIQUE

If you live with a drummer, you are accustomed to the sound of endless tapping on kitchen tables and denim thighs. Drummers breathe in meter, but even those of us who are not drummers are drawn to it, tapping our steering wheels to a radio beat. Meter gets in our blood.

Most readers will not consciously notice how writers handle sentence length and rhythm because rhythm should highlight meaning, not call attention to itself. Yet if we read prose with meter in mind, we will find editorials that end with a one-word punch and informational books that carefully repeat sentence patterns. The meter, or rhythm, of any piece of writing is its heartbeat.

Authors may use long sentences to show seemingly never-ending experiences or short ones to show fast action or freeze moments of time. In Bob Graham's *"Let's Get a Pup!" Said Kate* (2001), the story's rhythm matches its meaning when Kate's family tries to choose a dog at the animal shelter (note again the phrase mentioned in the previous lesson, "Experiment with Words").

> *They found fighters and biters, growlers and snarlers, short dogs, dogs long and thin, and dogs with their cheeks sucked in. They also found happy dogs, sad dogs, "take me" dogs, and dogs who couldn't care less. They saw smelly dogs, fat dogs, lean and mean dogs, chew-it-up-and-spit-it-out-at-you dogs, and dogs like walking nightmares.*
>
> *Then they saw . . . Dave.*

Discuss the pace of the first three sentences, each a long list. The sound of these listy sentences echoes the feeling of walking by the seemingly endless rows of cages at an animal shelter. Now note the last sentence: the large letters, the few words, the ellipsis. We slow down when we meet Dave, this perfect pup. Writers control sound and pace with punctuation and the lengths of sentences, and often this pace matches the action described.

Writing essays for WBFO, our local NPR station, helped me understand rhythm in prose. Knowing I would record these essays, I listened to the meters of my sentences, repeatedly reading my work aloud, revising sentences that sounded too slow, too choppy, too much like the last sentence I'd written. In "Once a Squirrel, Always a Squirrel" (2007), I wrote two versions of the same lead:

- You've seen me in your grocery store, the lady with sixteen cans of mushroom soup, seven boxes of Kleenex, and twenty pounds of rice. You thought that I just like soup, but really I'm a stockpiler. I'll say it again, admit it to you. I am a stockpiler.

- You've seen me in your grocery store. I'm that lady with sixteen cans of mushroom soup. Seven boxes of Kleenex. Twenty pounds of rice. You thought that I just like soup, but really I'm a stockpiler. I'll say it again, admit it to you. I. Am. A. Stockpiler.

The second version, the one I ultimately chose, slows a reader down with periods between each purchased item to emphasize my serious affliction: "I. Am. A. Stockpiler." Prose writers ask, "Where do I want readers to slow down? Speed up? How does this emphasize meaning?"

Students might think about meter only with respect to poetry, in terms of strict poetic forms such as sonnet, haiku, and sestina. However, varied rhythm is a part of daily speech and of story, information, and argument writing. Carefully considered, meter can create drama, focusing readers' attention on meaning.

Try It

While some poets adhere to formatted meter, many others invent their own meters or play with sound using line breaks and white space. To explore metered poetry with older students, choose one poem to study, and count both lines and syllables in lines, pointing out which words are stressed and which are not. Invite students to try writing a line or two imitating the rhythms you discover. Study the meters of several poems, discussing how the rhythms of various lines affect their meaning.

I listen to my writing in three ways: I read it aloud to myself, I ask someone else to read it to me (if the reader stumbles, it's my fault and I revise), and I record and listen to its sound. During drafting and revision, ask your students to listen to their own drafts, focusing on

- The sound of punctuation. Try different punctuation, as I did in the example above.

- Word order. Examine lists to see if the words might sound better in a different order.

- Word choices. Pay attention to lengths of words and consider whether a multisyllabic word or a short word fits a passage best.

- Sentence length. Experiment with combining simple sentences and breaking more complex ones apart, depending on whether the reader should read slowly or quickly.

Read the sentence-composing and story grammar books of Don and Jenny Killgallon, books such as *Story Grammar for Elementary School* (2008), books filled with ear-tuning and sentence-combining exercises.

Teach your students to respect their power as composer-writers. Writing is rhythm. Writing is music. Writing is speeding up and slowing down, singing to a reader like pattering rain. As Kristy Dempsey says, "To me, all writing is made to be read out loud, to be heard and even *performed!*"

STUDENT POEMS TO SHARE

Something's Up

Tic-Tic the seconds pass by,
Click-lock, Shut the door,
I feel like Something's up,
The rhythm of my heartbeat:

Thump!
Thump!
Thump!

Anxiety takes control,
Tapping my feet in nervous anticipation,
Tap! Tap!
Tippity! Tap!
Butterflies in my belly bubble up,
Panic rises sending shivers to my
fingertips,
The intercom buzzes,
words I feared to hear,
"Lock down!"
"Lock down!"
"This is not a drill!"
Now I Know Something's up.
Emily 6th grade

BASKET BALL

It's a fun sport
Confusing
Awesome
Never know when
Never know how
Anyone could chuck up a three
Anyone could brick it, or make it
Anyone could fall
Jump
Score
No one knows when
No one knows how.
By Thomas G.
Grade 4

Racing Round the Clock

The swiftly spinning second hand
advances sixty ticks.
The minute hand minutely marches on.
The hour hand holds mostly still
and hardly makes a twitch.
A clock's a sprint, a walk,
a marathon.

—*Allan Wolf*

© 2018 by Amy Ludwig VanDerwater, from *Poems Are Teachers*. Portsmouth, NH: Heinemann.

WORDS FROM THE POET

I've used alliteration *(repetition of sound) in "Racing Round the Clock" so that the words themselves, when read aloud, are reminiscent of the steady ticking of a clock. And I've given each hand of the clock a special sound: the second hand gets* s; *the minute hand gets* m; *and the hour hand gets* h.

All words have both music and meaning, sound and sense. That's true whether you are writing poetry or prose. Sometimes it just happens by accident. I use alliteration more for poetry than for prose. While writing prose I don't want the writing's sound to upstage the writing's sense. But in poetry, well, just about anything goes.

CONSIDER THE TECHNIQUE

Alliteration is the repetition of initial sounds in a series of words. If the sounds are consonants, we can call it *consonance*. If the repeated sounds are vowel sounds, the more specific name is *assonance*. But alliteration covers all. Children know alliteration from tongue twisters such as "Peter Piper picked a peck of pickled peppers" or "She sells seashells down by the seashore." Writers repeat words, symbols, and phrases, and so, too, do they repeat the initial sounds of words. This pleases readers' minds and ears.

When we read, our brains pay attention to stories and information, opinions and descriptions. We follow the subject. And at the same time, our mouths read along, aloud or quietly, and we hear the words in the air or in our heads, enjoying the way that sounds can circle back up upon themselves.

In Allan Wolf's poem, each unit of time seems to have its own voice thanks to the sounds he assigns to second, minute, and hour that mirror the first letter of each unit. In this way, Wolf brings sound and meaning together, each complementing the other. Three units of time, three sounds. And our mouths have great fun bouncing around from line to line, feeling the change in voice.

Wolf explains that he uses alliteration more liberally in poetry than in prose. We do, however, find brief examples of alliteration in all types of writing. Newspaper headlines and magazine and book titles such as *Hardwiring Happiness: The New Brain Science of Contentment, Calm, and Confidence* by Rick Hanson or *Lion's Lullaby* by Mij Kelly rely on repeated initial sounds to attract readers' attention. And authors in all genres play with alliteration as a way of making their texts feel good in the mouth and sound good to the ear. Again, sound. Alliteration is sound. Sound matters.

Wolf's reminder that "sometimes it just happens by accident" is important to remember. Serendipity is part of a writer's experience. As an oil painter layers with paint, writers layer words upon words, experimenting with new combinations, sometimes intentionally affecting their readers and sometimes surprising even themselves.

TRY IT

Take your students on a scavenger hunt for alliteration in a variety of texts—picture books, newspaper and magazine articles and headlines, chapter books, poetry. Look especially for more subtle examples that keep meaning at the forefront but enhance it through brief bursts of repeated sound. Copy alliterative sentences onto sentence strips or in the class' craft notebook, and talk about why an author might have chosen to repeat a particular sound. Alliteration does not live in a poetry cage; like all writing strategies and techniques, it runs wild in the genre landscape.

Students' experiments with alliteration will sometimes distract from their writing. Eager to select alliterative words, they may choose less-than-perfect meanings. The question to ask is, "Does this alliteration distract from the meaning of my text?" Writers must always be vigilant not to throw meaning by the wayside. No reader should be distracted by strange combinations of words that simply happen to begin with the letter *J*. Share Wolf's reminder: "While writing prose I don't want the writing's sound to upstage the writing's sense."

Welcome students to add alliteration to their notebook entries and drafts throughout the year, reminding them that just as with salt or garlic, too much of a good thing can ruin a whole dish. Encourage them to experiment with alliteration in small doses and not to leave readers with odd thoughts such as, "Wow! Look at the alliteration in this dead cat poem." Meaning first.

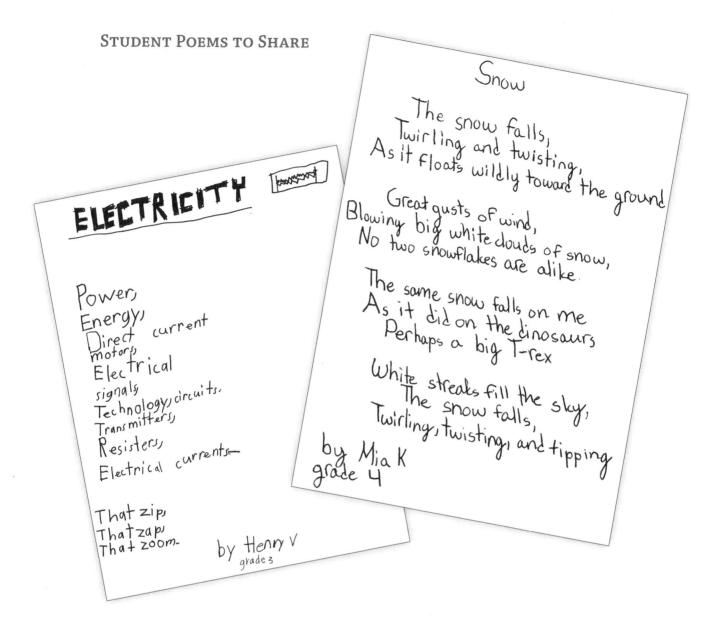

Snow

The snow falls,
Twirling and twisting,
As it floats wildly toward the ground

Great gusts of wind,
Blowing big white clouds of snow,
No two snowflakes are alike.

The same snow falls on me
As it did on the dinosaurs
Perhaps a big T-rex

White streaks fill the sky,
The snow falls,
Twirling, twisting, and tipping

by Mia K
grade 4

ELECTRICITY

Power,
Energy,
Direct current
motors,
Electrical
signals
Technology, circuits.
Transmitters,
Resisters,
Electrical currents

That zip,
That zap,
That zoom.

by Henry V
grade 3

Garbage Truck

Garbage Truck rumbles and booms down the street.
He snorts like a rhino and grunts like a boar.
He tosses the trash down his gullet to eat,
then gnashes and smashes and bellows for more.

Garbage Truck swaggers, he's brash and he's bold.
He snatches up cans with a *SLAM, BAM, CLANG, BASH!*
He tackles the smelly and battered and old.
He's the baron of bang and the master of crash.

Garbage Truck leaves with a roar and a brag.
The cans are all empty, a few fallen down.
With one final huff and a lost plastic bag
he blunders and thunders away through the town.

—*Kate Coombs*

WORDS FROM THE POET

My brother loved to follow garbage trucks down the street when he was five, which gave me the idea for this poem. Garbage trucks are loud, *so I used onomatopoeia, choosing words that make the sounds they describe. Some examples of onomatopoeia are words in comic books like* BAM! POW! THUD! *Or animal sounds like* oink, meow, moo. *Or words like* sizzle, snap, tick-tock. *How many onomatopoetic words can you find in "Garbage Truck"?*

CONSIDER THE TECHNIQUE

Onomatopoeia is when a word is made or invented by imitating a sound or noise from the actual world. The word's origin comes from Late Latin (*onomatopoeia*, 1570) and Greek (*onomatopoios*), and it means "the making of a name or word" (Dictionary.com 2017). Words based on their sounds are onomatopoetic.

When a baby imitates puppy yips or when you ask a toddler if he has to "tinkle," this is onomatopoeia. When I recall the annoying *BEEP* of our new coffeemaker or the whoosh of wind in the oak leaves, I bring onomatopoeia into my speech, allowing my friends to hear what I heard.

When a writer employs onomatopoeia, he brings the audio of a real-world scene into a text. When readers enter this text, the sounds of buzzing bees in a meadow or screeching chairs on tile floors fill their ears and offer a sound picture of a scene. Writing with onomatopoeia is another way to breathe life into a setting.

Onomatopoeia is a literary device used in all genres and in spoken language. Angela Johnson's picture book *Violet's Music* (2004) is a story structured through the various sounds that little Violet makes. From "Boom / Shake / Beat / Shake" near the start of the book to "Shake / TWANG / PLINK / Pluck / WHAH / WOO / YEAH!" on the very last page, readers are invited into the sound of Violet's life. Katherine Paterson's *Bridge to Terabithia* (1977) opens chapter 1 with "Ba-room, ba-room, ba-room, baripity, baripity, baripity—Good. His dad had the pickup going" (1). Before we even know the characters, we learn a little bit about them from the sounds coming from their tough-to-start truck.

Many onomatopoetic words are ordinary—like *boom* and *hiss*—but sometimes writers will change or stretch out letters in a word to emphasize sounds as in *squeeeeeeeeeak* or *zooooooom*. Occasionally, writers are inventors, making up new words with spellings that match the sounds of new or unusual experiences.

We often ask young writers to write "the movie you see in your mind." When we encourage them to write with onomatopoeia, we ask them to write "the movie you hear."

TRY IT

Play with onomatopoeia as a class by choosing a place that everyone knows. Together, draw quick sketches of this place: birdcage, basketball court, library, city street. Next, brainstorm the sounds in this place. Tell students that just as there is a difference between telling what a character said and letting her say it with dialogue, there is a difference between describing a sound (basketballs being thrown around) and an onomatopoetic sound (*bounce, boing, swoosh, slap*). Once you've developed a considerable list, ask students to sketch a new place, again brainstorming a list of sounds one might hear there. If they're interested, they might draft poems or setting descriptions of these places, including the onomatopoetic words. My poem "Forest Has a Song," from the book of the same title, is simply a list of woodsy sounds I have heard on forest hikes.

If you are fortunate enough to have bilingual students in your class or school community, talk about sound-effect words in multiple languages. Build a list of onomatopoetic words in English, and ask your bilingual students to share the counterparts from home languages. Say these words aloud together, noticing the similarities and differences.

To quickly find examples of onomatopoeia, read comic strips and graphic novels. You might also comb through favorite books or magazines looking for examples and considering when, how, and why authors use onomatopoeia.

Regardless of genre, encourage students to use onomatopoeia whenever they wish to let readers hear a place or animal or event.

My Room

I click and type
Creak back in my chair
Gasp, crash, boom!
I fall down

Doing my homework,
scribbling and scratching,
and just as I finish,
RIP!

My page tears,
I drop my pencil,
it clanks to the floor.

I flop onto my bed,
close my eyes.
Sighing, yawning,
I pickup the chair, plopping into it,
I click on the laptop, plug in my speakers,
type in the title
Music blasts on.
I relax

Kaiden B,
6th grade

the City

When
        You   See

the taxis pass you with a
swoosh
You know where you are.
        You see the huge
                Skyscrapers

and the honks of car horns
BEEP!

The elevator makes a little

    B I N G!
B

By Anna W.
Grade 3

5
....

Writers Craft
Beginnings and Endings

Beginnings and endings deserve special attention. Readers continue reading an op-ed or a picture book when the first lines are strong, and when the last lines are compelling, these readers walk away as if satisfied by a hearty meal. Our students, however, don't always understand this.

We raise our eyebrows when a student's piece begins, "My name is Jake, and this is my nonfiction book about whales." Or when a narrative ends, "I hope you liked reading this story. Come back next time!" But these students are making intelligent errors. When we meet someone on the street, we shake hands, say our names, and tell about ourselves. When we say goodbye, we offer words of kindness or a promise to meet again. If we consider that students are modeling their beginnings and endings on spoken conversation, these leads and conclusions make sense—they just don't work so well in writing.

In life, we teach children specific strategies for day-to-day beginnings and endings, reminding them to iron their clothes to make a good first impression and to break up in person rather than by text. So, too, can we offer specific techniques for beginning and ending pieces of writing across genres. All authors work from a fistful of strategies when beginning and ending pieces. These are not secrets. We can study leads and conclusions in poems, apprenticing ourselves to authors, ironing our beginnings and breaking up gracefully at the end of our own written texts.

Learn to Craft Beginnings and Endings from Poems

Poems all begin, and poems all end, and they often do both on the same page. A writer interested in beginnings and endings can easily study how the lead and conclusion of the same text work together. Sometimes a poem ends as it began, and sometimes it begins with a startle. Sometimes a poem starts with a description, and sometimes it ends by funneling down to one word.

Writers of all genres use similar techniques for entering and leaving texts. In this chapter, we'll explore a few such possibilities, but you will find others as you read in different genres. You might make a chart or scrapbook page of "Interesting Beginnings" and "Memorable Endings." Look for texts that lead with a sound effect or an author's internal thought. Notice when a text ends with a call to action for readers or a summary of important ideas. Pay attention when a book closes quietly, painting one final image onto a reader's mental canvas. Anything we observe and admire as readers—in beginnings and endings and elsewhere—we can try as writers.

Math

"Asians are supposed to be good at math."
Mr. Chao can't figure me out.
"Asians are quiet. Asians like numbers."
Me, I like to shout.

—*Janet Wong*

WORDS FROM THE POET

Mr. Lau, my high school Algebra 2 teacher, approached me after class one day with a puzzled and pained look on his face. He said: "I don't understand. You're Asian. You're supposed to be good at math! Are you spending enough time on homework?" I stood there dumbfounded and disappointed that Mr. Lau, an American-born Chinese like me, was pushing this traditional stereotype. Yet I have accidentally said insensitive and racist things at times, too. I believe that most of us are guilty of this; the challenge is admitting it when you make a mistake. And yes: I am indeed terrible at many forms of math, but I am pretty great at estimating the number of beans in a jar.

We all have moments when we are surprised by something someone says to us. Maybe we're speechless because we're overjoyed by a compliment; maybe we're stunned in disbelief by hurtful words. Using those words in a quote at the beginning of a poem is a great way to deal with statements that surprise us. It's also a great way to figure out how we feel about a situation. My poem "Math" is an example of this.

CONSIDER THE TECHNIQUE

Beginning a piece of writing with dialogue kicks a text off with one very specific voice. A reader asks, "Who is speaking? What is happening?" Dropped into the middle of a scene, listening to someone speak, a reader must immediately get his bearings, and so the writer has grabbed the reader's attention. When I first read Janet Wong's "Math," Mr. Chao's opening statement made me wonder, "Who would say this?" and I kept reading.

Mildred D. Taylor begins her historical novel *Roll of Thunder, Hear My Cry* (1976) with dialogue: "Little Man, would you come on? You keep it up and you're gonna make us late" (3). Only one sentence in, and we know we're in a hurry. Similarly, in a famous chapter beginning, E. B. White opens *Charlotte's Web* (1952) with Fern saying, "Where's Pa going with that ax?" (1).

Sometimes writers begin with the words of others, not as dialogue but as quotes spoken in other times and places. Kathleen Krull's "Marie Curie" chapter in her nonfiction *Lives of the Scientists: Experiments, Explosions (and What the Neighbors Thought)* (2013) begins, "'Be less curious about people and more curious about ideas,' warned the woman who might have thrown this book out the window" (55). This quote is more distant than dialogue, situating a reader and text in a larger conversation.

Reflecting on the words of people in our lives, Wong reminds us, "We all have moments when we are surprised by something someone says to us." The voices of others create the soundtracks of our lives; they are a kind of music, and beginning with dialogue is a way to wave readers into a text and perk up their ears. What did someone say? Start there.

Try It

Share a bit of dialogue that has stayed with you for some reason. For example, when my father knew either my sister or I was confronted with a moral dilemma, he'd say, "You know what a Ludwig would do." I could easily begin a narrative with these words from my dad, following with the story of a decision I once made. Students might remember bits of dialogue that

- they recall from early childhood
- stay with them for some reason
- they have heard over and over again
- made them feel a big feeling, either good or bad

Part of a writer's work is to explore various topics, and one way to do this is to designate pages in notebooks to capture spoken language. Encourage your students to pay attention and listen for interesting dialogue as others speak. You might invite students to list a variety of places and for each one, list bits of dialogue they have heard or overheard in these places. For example, years ago, while waiting in line at the Gap, I heard one teenage girl say to another, "My mother always told me that every girl needs a good pair of ice skates." I've often thought that that would be a great lead for a novel. Why would a mother say this?

Students might each copy a bit of remembered dialogue atop a new page, and then write long from it. Nudge them to write to the bottom of the page, to see what emerges. As Wong says, "Using those words in a quote at the beginning of a poem is a great way to deal with statements that surprise us. It's also a great way to figure out how we feel about a situation."

If students are in the midst of drafting narratives, study stories that begin with the words of characters, giving students time to write dialogue leads of their own.

Surprise, Surprise

Colby Pointed:
"Look it's Sunday! The rescue dogs are here!
Can We
Go check 'em out?"

MY Stomach turned
MY heart jumped
Since
My
Dog
Died
I was
Afraid.

"Are you okay with that Peyton?"

"Yep." I Sighed Softly
SURPRISE, SURPRISE.

Colby pointed
one out.
"I like that one!" he exlaimed
Golden brown
Very cute
I actually like her
SURPRISE SURPRISE.

"Do You want her?" Mom asked

"Yes" We both exlaimed.
SURPRISE, SURPRISE.

Now,
Our hearts have SAWYER!!

    - By Peyton K
        Grade 3

On Stage

"Places, everyone. Places!"
The show is about to begin.
My stomach turns
            over and over
like a ferris wheel
            I can't escape.
I must go on
    to play my part.
The music starts,
    the lights go up,
            and now,
        we're on.
A million thoughts race
    through my mind
like rabbits chasing
            through
                a field:
Is my voice loud enough?
Will I forget my cue?
And if I do,
Will I cause commotion?
Will I fall off stage?
But bit by bit,
    I play my part.
    I hit my cues.
    I get some laughs.
    I'm having fun!
And then, APPLAUSE!
My moment, frozen in time.
I'd live there forever
        if I could,
but I can't because...
The show must go on!   by Kate D.
                        Grade 7

Sophie

In the library I slept
    dreaming of dragons
I read about in my bed the night before
    staying up late, so late to explore
        dark caves piled with sapphires and pearls
        and shining silver scales skimming
            shining golden worlds
    to smell the smoky choking breath
        as fire crackled in my hair
It felt, oh how it felt like I was there
In the library I slept
    dreaming of dragons
till Ms. Kagan woke me
    buzzing in my ear,
"Sophie, my dear, it's book time.
    Catch those z's at home."
I tried to grab a wing, a tail
    but they were gone, without a trace
I tell you school is not the place
    when you like to sleep in company
        but you like to read alone

Tanya

Hot cocoa warm and brown
    the library is my place
to cozy down
    and fly or sail or ride away
One day checking out moon rocks
    the next, searching for the Golden Fleece
One hour giving myself goosebumps
    another, bump-bump-bumping by a flock of geese
And oh the folks I meet
    sour, sweet
    smart and dumb
They welcome me
    I welcome them
Mi casa es su casa
    Your house is mine
And any place where I can read
    is home

    —Marilyn Singer

WORDS FROM THE POET

In my book All We Needed to Say: Poems About School from Tanya and Sophie, *the two main characters have opposing attitudes toward school. We see them in a number of rooms and situations throughout the day. Tanya is a happy camper. Sophie isn't. But both love books. In this pair of poems, I put both girls in the library. They relate very differently to the place. But neither character's point of view is "right" or "wrong." I think that setting the scene with specificity at the beginning of a poem invites a reader inside that scene. The setting also suggests images that the characters (and the writer) use to describe their circumstances. I live across from an elementary school, so I've met quite a few Tanyas and Sophies. And I've been inside many a library. I'd say in that room, I'm more of a Tanya!*

CONSIDER THE TECHNIQUE

"Where am I?" One way to begin a piece of writing is to place your reader in a place—right at the start. It's a bit like saying, "Plop! Here you are. Have a look and listen." And as Marilyn Singer explains, "I think that setting the scene with specificity at the beginning of a poem invites a reader inside that scene." A writer leading with setting creates a specific tone within the first few lines, all based on what setting details she chooses to highlight.

We are all familiar with picture books and chapter books that begin with setting. Mary Lyn Ray's picture book *Welcome, Brown Bird* (2004) begins with month and place and nature imagery: "A boy lived at the edge of a hemlock woods. In March he watched the snow melt. In April he saw the grass grow green. Then he began to listen."

Leading with setting is common in other genres too. In her *This I Believe* essay "Serving and Saving Humanity" (2009), journalist Molly Bingham opens with, "When you are sitting alone in a cold, dusty six-by-nine-foot concrete prison cell with nothing but a wool blanket and the constant fear of death, you think. A lot." Her readers are suddenly in prison too.

Information texts often begin with setting. In his *National Geographic Kids* article "Penguin City" (2017), Scott Elder leads with

> *A sprawling city bustles with the loud racket of morning rush hour. Crowds of commuters hurry past each other, skirting by construction sites. Suddenly one traveler bumps into another and sets off a shouting match. (14)*

Before telling us we're in Antarctica visiting chinstrap penguins, Elder allows us to see and hear our surroundings.

When writers start with setting, they may name a particular place or simply describe it, allowing readers to discover where they are. Writers often name the time of day—by actual time or by placement of sun or moon in the sky. Or they describe details of weather, the way the raindrops dribble down car windows, the faint rainbow over an apartment building. Writers dip into the paint box of the senses, beginning with a clink of spoons on ceramic mugs (sound) or a hint of jasmine in the air (smell). Sometimes writers describe the way light falls on trees or the way shadows play against a wall.

TRY IT

Teach your students to write setting leads by asking them to first consider the content of their writing. Encourage them to ask themselves, "What tone do I hope to create in my first few lines?" An opinion piece about children and screen time might begin with a description of a silent and empty playground. A memoir about a great-grandmother might lead with a description of her long-ago kitchen, apple pies cooling on every surface.

Ask your students to think about which particular details of setting are most relevant to their meaning. Remind them to consider

- time of day
- objects within sight
- weather
- how the light falls
- how the air feels
- sounds
- smells

To practice writing setting leads, consider having students all write descriptions of the same place, but with different tones and meanings in mind. For example, students might each describe a veterinarian's office from the point of view of a different person (or animal):

- a pet owner taking a new puppy for its first wellness visit
- a person allergic to dogs
- a pet owner visiting with a sick dog
- a brand-new vet
- a pet owner visiting to have an old, beloved dog put to sleep
- a dog or cat or bunny

Ask students to read each other's setting leads and discuss the varied ways they have described the same place based on meaning. Which details did different writers choose to convey tone right at the start? You might try a similar exercise by asking students to each describe the same place, this time not giving specifics. Again, share and discuss. What can you infer about meaning based on how each writer uses specific setting details?

You might even have your young writers add line breaks to different setting leads or place descriptions. The addition of a few line breaks and some carefully chosen repetition can quickly turn prose into poetry.

STUDENT POEMS TO SHARE

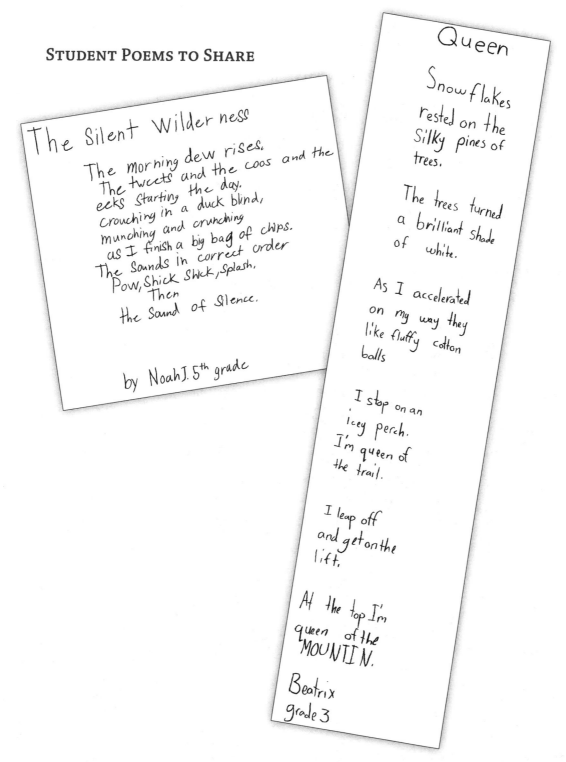

The Silent Wilderness

The morning dew rises,
The tweets and the coos and the
eeks starting the day.
crouching in a duck blind,
munching and crunching
as I finish a big bag of chips.
The sounds in correct order
Pow, Shick Shick, Splash,
Then
the sound of silence.

by Noah J. 5th grade

Queen

Snowflakes
rested on the
silky pines of
trees.

The trees turned
a brilliant shade
of white.

As I accelerated
on my way they
like fluffy cotton
balls

I stop on an
icey perch.
I'm queen of
the trail.

I leap off
and get on the
lift.

At the top I'm
queen of the
MOUNTIN.

Beatrix
grade 3

Still Stuck on You

When first I fell for a banana slug
all my friends would say was, "Ugh."

It started as friendship: he simply was lost,
stuck on the sidewalk he'd tried to cross.
Who could resist—his whole body smiled!
His freckles alone, they had me beguiled.

The slug had no one to call a friend,
and me? I needed a pet to attend.

I loved to follow his shimmery trails.
He charmed me with tales of infamous snails.
While gladly listening, he let *me* do the talking.
Glued on and glistening, he let *me* do the walking,

One day, I kissed him (I think on his hips),
and his slime—who knew?—it numbed my lips!

I sensed that my sluggish love was ill-fated,
doomed even before we had dated.
All that was left to do was admit it—
but by then, my banana slug had split-ed.

—*Michael J. Rosen*

© 2018 by Amy Ludwig VanDerwater, from *Poems Are Teachers*. Portsmouth, NH: Heinemann.

WORDS FROM THE POET

All my poems start with not-knowing, rather than knowing. So the writing itself fuels the finding out, feeds the wondering and wandering. The goal is to stumble onto something, not to simply describe what's in plain sight.

Often I'll start with a quirky premise: a conjoining of two elements that catches me off guard so that, instead of having an easy solution ("Oh! Oh, I know!"), I find myself puzzled ("Oh, wow . . . now what?") and challenged.

In this poem, one of several I've written about "regrettable pets," I imagined what would happen if a human fell for a slimy, yellow, banana-shaped, shell-less snail. Discovering tidbits of natural history, I doggedly followed where they led . . . eventually recognizing the possibilities of a poem that I could then shape.

CONSIDER THE TECHNIQUE

"Wait! Fell for a *banana slug*?" Who falls for banana slugs? You must read on.

Beginning with a startle or shock is one way to quickly bring readers into a text. This is the cold-water-in-the-face approach, and it will certainly wake readers out of mindless skimming.

We find this type of beginning in all genres. Consider these examples:

- Neil Gaiman, *The Graveyard Book* (2008): "The knife had a handle of polished black bone, and a blade finer and sharper than any razor. If I sliced you, you might not even know you had been cut, not immediately" (1).

- Barbara Park, *Mick Harte Was Here* (1996): "I don't want to make you cry. I just want to tell you about Mick. But I thought you should know right up front that he's not here anymore" (4).

- My eldest daughter's college essay: "I grew up without a TV."

- Susan Hood, *Ada's Violin: The Story of the Recycled Orchestra of Paraguay* (2016): "Ada Ríos grew up in a town made of trash."

Each of these beginnings startles, but for different reasons. They are frightening (Gaiman), sad (Park), curious (VanDerwater), surprising (Hood).

Startling leads offer readers a promise at the get-go: "This will be good." They shift the reader's mood, grabbing him by the arm, yanking his eyes down the page. As writers, we too can begin our pieces with a startle, can begin with our most silly, surprising, shocking, or upsetting fact or statement.

TRY IT

Ask your students to identify the most startling fact or statement they have to share about their topics, and then have them experiment using these as leads. This is especially effective with content-area writing, such as science (female praying mantises eat males' heads after mating) or history (there existed a secret interrogation center at Fort Hood during World War II). From their reading and research, students can list the most startling facts they find, choosing one to begin a short notebook entry or draft.

Students might also list startling statements and realizations about their own lives or about the lives of people they know or have invented: "My parents do not speak to each other" or "My family has eleven cats." These, too, can make excellent starts to essays, short stories, bits of memoir. Try inviting students to craft leads by bringing two surprising things together, as Rosen does: "Often I'll start with a quirky premise: a conjoining of two elements that catches me off guard."

Collect good examples of leads that startle, and as students revise drafts with attention to leads, remind them to consider the following variations of the startling statement as possibilities:

- unusual sound effect

- seemingly unbelievable quote

- heartbreaking line

- silly statement

- uncommon opinion

- shocking fact

Spirit

I am alone for life.
All by myself.
My mother and father's spirit
Stays with me though

The wind
In the sandy hills
Is the only sound.
Filling the dusty air.

My mother and father's spirit
Burns
In my memory.

By Nina Grade 4

I listen as I hear the door
tearing off our camp.

A huge earthquake hits and we
are dumped into an
enormous crater.

We wait, all piled up as a
vanilla-white liquid
submerges us.

We shout in joy as a
silver rescue craft
lifts us up into a
big
dark
cave.

Crunch!

A day in the life of
a cheerio.

By James P.
grade 5

Yes, Boys Can Dance!

I love hip hop, tap, and jazz,
but what about ballet, is it really okay
for boys to spin and twirl?

When I ask Mamá, she shows me a photo
of Carlos Acosta, who leaps so high
when he plays the brave knight, Don Quixote,
that he is known as The Flying Cuban.

That could be me someday, a muscular man
in midair
who soars as smoothly
as a superhero . . .

but only if I study and practice, Papá warns,
so now is the time to start slowly learning,
earthbound at first, while my dance wings
grow.

—*Margarita Engle*

WORDS FROM THE POET

How do I write question poems? I daydream and ask my own questions. In this poem, I've imagined a boy wondering about gender roles in traditional dance forms. He is able to answer his own questions by learning about groundbreaking role models, such as José Limón, the great Mexican American pioneer of male roles in modern dance, and Carlos Acosta, "The Flying Cuban" who made history as the London Ballet's first black Romeo.

Some of the research for answering my question came a bit later, after my initial wondering. Sometimes when writing, I simply ask relaxed, daydreamy questions, and then I switch back to busy mode, investigating my questions by finding information at the library or online. Finally, I come back to that quiet place, finishing my first draft while daydreaming (visualizing!) the answer in action, whether it is a dancer in motion or any other wonderful surprise.

CONSIDER THE TECHNIQUE

When a writer begins a text with a question—"is it really okay / for boys to spin and twirl?"—readers cannot help but consider the question themselves. Of course, in Margarita Engle's poem, the title, "Yes, Boys Can Dance!," actually answers the question she poses in the lead—an interesting technique for titling.

A story might begin with an internal question or a question for a character or for readers. In Jennifer Niven's YA novel *All the Bright Places* (2016), the narrator, Finch, asks herself, "Is today a good day to die?" (3). Trudy Ludwig's picture book *The Invisible Boy* (2013) poses her lead question to readers: "Can you see Brian, the invisible boy?"

A nonfiction writer may begin with a fact-based question, such as "Why does an octopus have eight hearts?" sharing a little-known but fascinating fact. And in opinion writing, an author might lead with a question or two related to the topic. Take Teresa Carr's article "Off-Label Use: Should Drugs Do Double Duty?" (2017) on the *Consumer Reports* website, which begins, "Nervous about giving a big presentation? Your doctor might prescribe a blood pressure drug like generic propranolol to calm you. Can't sleep? You might leave the doctor's office with a prescription for. . . ." By placing readers in specific situations through questioning, Carr begins convincing us of her opinion with her very first words. Note, too, how she asks and answers two questions in a row. Anne Schreiber does this in her nonfiction book *Pandas* (2010): "Look! Up in the tree! Is it a cat? Is it a raccoon? No! It's a **Giant Panda**!" (4).

An author may lead with a moral or hypothetical question, placing readers in a possible situation or asking them to align with a viewpoint. In John Rosemond's parenting column titled "In a Family, Parents' Relationship Comes First" (2016), Rosemond begins, "I recently asked a married couple who have three kids, none of whom are yet teens, 'Who are the most important people in your family?'"

Regardless of the type of question asked in the lead, questions make readers think about possible answers, engaging them on page or line one.

TRY IT

Margarita Engle asks, "How do I write question poems? I daydream and ask my own questions." This emphasis on daydreaming and wonder is important. With this in mind, before students write in their notebooks, offer them time to daydream here and there, closing eyes, inviting questions. This will help students find ideas, and it will also offer possible leads.

To practice question beginnings, ask your students to each select a notebook entry. Model how to write new beginnings to these entries, experimenting with question leads. Try asking a question

- of your reader using the second person *you*

- of yourself, musing inside your own head

- with a surprising answer

- with no right or wrong answer

- involving facts

- that poses a moral or an ethical question

- or two in a row, answering them (or not).

This is not a one-day lesson but rather a strategy writers can return to throughout their writing lives. By keeping a list of technique possibilities, students will come to see that a writer-dance-move such as starting with a question is timeless and genre-less.

Can Animals Dream

Can animals dream?
If they could dream
what would they dream about?
Getting a new home?
Getting new friends?
Being free?
Hiding?
Running?
Can animals dream?

By: Ridge M.
Grade 2

Autism

The start of the day
is like the start of the game
or is it a challenge
can I win?
We are all different, none the same
Some of us have problems
of different kinds
So many faces I cannot read
sad or happy
happy or sad?
The long lights are like the
blinding sun making my head hurt
The teachers want to meet with me
I want to go home
The day is over, too many sounds...
Finally home.

by Samantha B.
Grade 4

Poem for a Bully

Somewhere deep inside you
there's a softer, kinder place.
I know this will surprise you—
but I've seen it in your face.
Your eyes are often sad, although
you wear a surly grin.
Sometimes when you stand all alone
your "mean" seems worn and thin.
I wish that you would take a step—
a small, but brave one too—
and look inside yourself to find
the good I see in you.

—*Eileen Spinelli*

WORDS FROM THE POET

It is easy to look at a bully in a dark light. To write him or her off. I wanted to go deeper. I wanted my poem to speak to some hidden spark of goodness. I wanted my poem to speak of hope. End your story or poem by answering the question you started with— and don't just tell us, make us feel *the answer as a ripple in the heart.*

CONSIDER THE TECHNIQUE

I will never forget the night when our nine-year-old came downstairs past bedtime. I scolded, "You should be in bed!"

Softly, holding back sobs, he asked, "Mom? Have you ever read *Stone Fox*?"

I went to him, knowing. "Yes. It's a real crier."

He kept on, "But Mom. The ending. Do you remember what happened at the end?" Henry described in perfect detail the last scene of this short chapter book by John Reynolds Gardiner, now branded on his young heart. And he sobbed. I did too. Six years later, I still believe that the ending of John Reynolds Gardiner's *Stone Fox* made our child—and me—a bit kinder. The ending. The heart tug.

Sometimes an essay leaves us angry or wistful and an article may leave us brokenhearted, leading us to volunteer or send donations or write to our senators. Writing changes our hearts and our actions, and writers are aware of this power. Dave Philipps closes his *New York Times* article "Troops Who Cleaned Up Radioactive Islands Can't Get Medical Care" (2017) with a quote from veteran Jeff Dean: "'No one seems to want to admit anything,' Mr. Dean said. 'I don't know how much longer we can wait, we have guys dying all the time.'" Philipps says no more, just leaves Dean's words in the air.

Of her poem, Eileen Spinelli writes, "I wanted my poem to speak of hope." And at the end, readers hold onto the kindness of the speaker, this hope that Spinelli planted. Jacqueline Woodson offers such hope in her picture book *The Other Side*, as readers see the possibility of tearing down fences between people. Conversely, Woodson's *Each Kindness* (2012) ends with regret and sadness hanging in the air. Writers know what they want "to speak of" and often include this emotion at the end of texts, leaving us thinking. Our hearts have been zipped open with words.

Facts are important. Feelings are important too. In all kinds of texts, writers pay attention to readers' emotions, often tucking us in and saying good-bye with a hint of joy, a whiff of sadness, a spark of anger. Ending with emotion is one way to ensure that our words linger like perfume long after they are read.

TRY IT

Remind students of times when finishing a class book or poem or article made them feel a big feeling. "Remember how we all cried? Remember how we all wrote letters because we were angry?" Share stories of times you have felt deep feelings after reading, feelings of joy or sadness, anger or hope. Students can find these texts and study the last lines, asking, "What did this writer do to make me feel this way?" Copy heart-tug endings you find in books and collect them in a small basket or in your class craft notebook.

Invite students to write about subjects they have strong feelings about. Again, start by listing some emotions: grief, peace, joy, surprise, despair, amazement. Ask students to each choose one of these and write for a few minutes about a moment when each of them felt this way. Encourage them to use dialogue and inner thoughts and actions to show these feelings in just a few sentences.

Now, have students work backward. Write about what led up to this climactic moment. Experiment in notebooks with writing *toward* an emotional ending, leaving readers with the scene that paints sadness or elation.

Encourage students to regularly dive back into their drafts, considering their endings, asking, "Might I close this piece with a heart tug?"

"The Secret Annex"

The stairs were steep
My thoughts were heavy,
wonder,
curiosity,
Fear
filled my head;

A bookshelf hid the unknown stairs
like the Secret Annex hid the Franks;

standing in the Annex, such dim light, how do they live
so little space,
this way
for two years??

A small window in the attic
their only source of sunlight;

Pictures carefully placed on a wall, movie stars and cartoons,
the dreams of a fourteen year old girl;

Robbed of fresh air
and freedom
but never robbed
of hope.

By: Eliza L.
Grade 7

Home

There used to be a home for me
There were parents
There was a sister
I usually watched TV on the sofa.

One day
I left my home
And it disappeared,
My memories,
My histories...

I came back to home
But there was no one

Except one letter...
on the old desk,
"I love you, son"
And the water started to fall off to the

old floor.
It was not water
It was tears

by Erick S.
Grade 6

Cabin of One Hundred Lights

Deep
    deep
        deep

in the wild,
wild woods

near the cabin
near the cabin
that they call one hundred lights
(some are candles, some are lanterns,
only seen on windy nights . . .)

there's a path
        path
            path
of pine, pine, pine
down a gnarly, twisted trail
with a bent and broken sign,

and somewhere in the dark
is an old, old owl, who *whoo whoo* hoots
near a crooked brown vine

as the wind gets wilder
and the sky's complaint
is hammering thunder
and the conversation's faint

we look into the windows
(legends lurking in the air)
and we feel the slightest brushing
of a someone not quite there

who is
    deep
        deep
            deep
in the wild
wild woods

near the cabin
near the cabin
that they call one hundred lights . . .

—*Rebecca Kai Dotlich*

WORDS FROM THE POET

When I began to write the poem "Cabin of One Hundred Lights" I realized immediately that I wanted it to be a circular poem, which means essentially that it would end in a way similar to the way it began. This can be done with repetition of words, phrases, and sounds. I felt this might visually and emotionally take the reader really deep, and deeper still, into the woods, coupled with a mysterious feel, and add a concrete element of actually circling the cabin just as the young explorers were.

CONSIDER THE TECHNIQUE

Upon meeting someone new, we might shake hands or give cheek kisses. After a few pleasantries or a lengthy conversation, when it is time to leave, we shake hands or give cheek kisses again. This ritual cements our meeting, and somehow the second handshake or kiss is different from the first. Now we know each other; now we are linked. Our lives and the world of nature offer such repeated circles. Pack the car before going to Grandma's; unpack the car upon returning home. Sunrise; sunset.

Journalists and essayists, storytellers and poets know that readers like to "walk out the same door they walked in." Writers of all genres connect leads with endings in powerful ways, creating circular texts. In the picture book *City Dog, Country Frog* by Mo Willems, it is springtime at both beginning and end, each with a different animal having lost and now seeking a friend. "Twinkle Twinkle Little Star" begins and ends with the same two lines: "Twinkle twinkle little star, / How I wonder what you are."

Some circular texts end with the exact same words as the opening words. In others, the ending somehow echoes the beginning, repeating a few key words or ideas but changing them somehow, indicating that here at the end, something is the same—but something is different too. Katherine Applegate's nonfiction picture book *Ivan: The Remarkable True Story of the Shopping Mall Gorilla* (2014) is a good example. Page one reads, "In leafy calm, in gentle arms, a gorilla's life began." Then, after Ivan is stolen, transported to live in a shopping mall for several years, and finally brought to a sanctuary, the story closes, "In leafy calm, in gentle arms, a gorilla's life began again." The circle closes, and the addition of one word—*again*—echoes and yet changes the meaning.

In his *New Yorker* opinion piece "Where the Second Avenue Subway Went Wrong" (2017), James Surowiecki leads with

> *On New Year's Eve, at a party to celebrate the opening of the long-awaited Second Avenue subway, Governor Andrew Cuomo said the project showed that government "can still do big things and great things." What he didn't say is that the project also shows that government can do really expensive things.*

He ends with these two lines, repeating Cuomo's words but with a caveat: "It's good for government to do big things, great things. But it's better if it can do them under budget." Same words. But after reading Surowiecki's opinions, the reader finds a different meaning in them at the end.

TRY IT

Once your students are aware of circular texts, they will find them everywhere. When they do, discuss why authors of different genres might begin and end pieces the same way:

- to show change

- to show how something has stayed the same

- to press an important point through repetition

- to bring a reader back to a previous setting or quote

You might model writing a circular beginning and ending with a piece (in any genre) you have already written. As you model, think aloud about questions such as "How might I connect my beginning and ending?" and "Which line in this piece would work well as both lead and conclusion?" Show students how you experiment with a few different ways to write this line, playing with wording and length, or perhaps keeping your circular line exactly the same.

Encourage students to try a circular structure in their writing if they wish to leave their readers with an echo. As your students' drafts progress, ask them to reread their beginnings considering, "Is there anything in my lead that I might carry into my conclusion?"

No Rules For Art

Art Art Art
there are no
Rules For Art
Art Art I love
Art it is so
so so so
colerfull
there is no Rules
For Art. I can
do wat ever I
won't it is so
messy and I
see happynes
in the colers
and
you
can
write
wa't
ever
you
feel
huray huray art
makes me so happy
you can draw or write
the colers you can
do wat ever I wont
there are no Rules For Art. by Madelyn grade 2

Sound

Sound is a whisper
of a small bird

Ready to spread its wings
Knowing the Father
will protect his young

Sound is a silent hallway
but becomes loud
when the children run through
Not caring what will happen next

Sound is a pencil
writting the next hit song
as the writer hums to the planned
beat

Sound is a whisper,
a very slight whisper

by Leia Z, grade 5

Brave

Red means stop.
Look both ways.
I am not afraid.

Sleepovers.
School bus rides.
I am not afraid.

Escalators.
Wiggle teeth.
Thunderstorms.
Roller coasters.
Movie monsters.
Scraped up knees.
I am not afraid.

SPIDERS!

—*Sara Holbrook*

WORDS FROM THE POET

What's new, exciting, and fun all over? A surprise! Artists, poets, and musicians use patterns, repeated rhythms and phrases. Patterns in poetry enable readers to anticipate and predict what's next. But who wants to always be predictable? Instead, after my first draft, I go back and challenge myself to take an unusual turn in the poem. Sometimes I rearrange lines or the words within a line. Or sometimes I'll try to take the pattern I've set up and break it in the last line. SURPRISE!

CONSIDER THE TECHNIQUE

Each of us has had the experience of knowing how a book or movie would end. And it's satisfying ("I'm so smart!") to figure out an ending. Yet sometimes, an ending takes us by surprise. We never saw that ending coming, and mouth open, we may shake our heads or laugh out loud. There's an element of joy in being surprised by an author.

Young children know about surprise endings from patterned oral stories such as "It Was a Dark, Dark Night (There was a GHOST!)" and patterned picture books like the funny *Tadpole's Promise* by Jeanne Willis. In this book, a tadpole professes his love to a caterpillar, urging her to never change. Well, nature requires change, and so caterpillar becomes butterfly as tadpole becomes frog. Even though we readers know these scientific facts, we are amazed when, on the final page, frog unknowingly eats his former love, now a butterfly. "How could this happen?" Our eyes grow wide.

In Remy Charlip's patterned picture book *Fortunately,* a character alternates between feeling fortunate and unfortunate, ultimately feeling happy to end up at a surprise party for him. As the main character is surprised on that last party page, so are readers. Charlip builds up scene after scene of anxiety and wonder to relieve them all with a great joyful surprise at the end. In pattern books like these, authors do what Holbrook explains: "Or sometimes I'll try to take the pattern I've set up and break it in the last line. SURPRISE!"

A story need not be patterned in order to surprise at the end. Consider the ending of John Green's *The Fault in Our Stars* (spoiler alert), when Hazel Grace is surprised by the death of her love, Augustus Waters. In a book such as this, the author does not set up and break a pattern but rather creates a story line with an unforeseen ending. If a reader reads a story like this a second time, he might discover clues he missed on a first read. When crafting such endings, writers must write both toward the expected and unexpected ending at once.

Reading the surprise ending of a text is a little bit like finding a beautiful blue piece of sea glass as you stroll along a lakeshore. For an hour you only find little stones and bits of brown glass, bits of clear glass—and then at last, blue. As writers, we can offer readers this last giggle, this last aha, this last wow.

TRY IT

Students will likely recognize surprise endings in their reading before they write surprise endings themselves. Begin by talking about times that you have been surprised in life. I might talk about the time Mark jumped out at me when I walked into the kitchen. If I write about this and want my reader to be surprised, just as I was, I could write the ending first, drafting my last line as "Mark jumped out from behind the door!" Have students try this, writing a moment of surprise in one line, at the bottoms of their papers. Then write toward this line, in either narrative or poetry form.

Or try Sara Holbrook's suggestion and ask your students to draft a piece with a distinct pattern. Notice together how her poem is a list with the repeating line "I am not afraid," and share Sara's words, "But who wants to always be predictable. . . . I go back and challenge myself to take an unusual turn." Make a pattern. Break it. This is what writers do—offer the unexpected.

You might think of this technique as the inside out of "Start with a Startle." Instead of startling readers at the get-go, though, this time you startle them at the finish line.

STUDENT POEMS TO SHARE

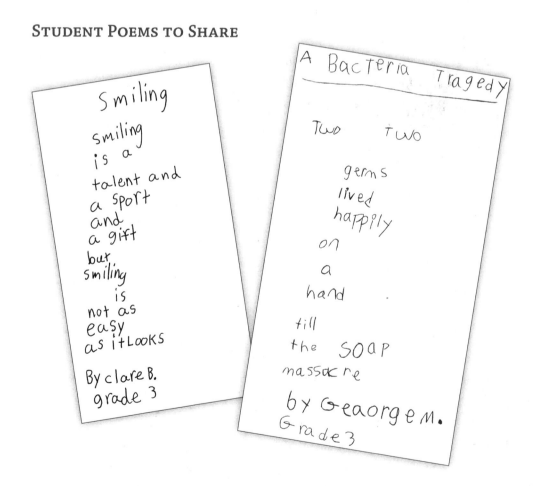

Smiling

smiling
is a
talent and
a sport
and
a gift
but
smiling
is
not as
easy
as it looks

By clare B.
grade 3

A Bacteria Tragedy

Two   Two

germs
lived
happily
on
a
hand
till
the soap
massacre

by Geaorge M.
Grade 3

Little Cat

Little cat, little cat, where did you go?
You were gone the whole night and I missed you so.

Where were you during the thunder and lightning?
Oh dear little cat, how it must have been frightening.

Did you find a safe place that was toasty and warm,
A cozy snug shelter to weather the storm?

Or were you alone on the dark lonely street,
With no one to pet you and nothing to eat?

And how did you find your way back to our nest,
To curl up on the lap of the one you love best?

Oh little cat, little cat, where did you go?
I wish you could tell me, but I'll never know.

—*Lesléa Newman*

WORDS FROM THE POET

I am often inspired to write a poem because a question is nagging me. Sometimes the question is answered by writing the poem. Other times the question remains unanswered and the poem leaves readers with a sense of mystery and an invitation to use their imaginations. Such is the case with "Little Cat."

CONSIDER THE TECHNIQUE

There are some things humans will never know. In studies of the environment, local news, and people of long ago, as well as in questions of religion, personal choices, and outer space, our world is filled with uncertainty. Since writing often mirrors living, writers sometimes choose to leave their readers wondering at the end, just as we are frequently left wondering in life.

I am reminded of a recent winter day when I read aloud the persuasive picture book *Hey, Little Ant* by Phillip and Hannah Hoose (1998) to a class of third graders. This is a story book, and it is a story book structured as a conversation between a boy who wishes to step on an ant and the ant himself. The boy wants to kill; the ant wants to live. And in a volley of rhymed chatter, each takes turns trying to convince the other of his opinion. As I read, I could tell these young listeners wanted to know what would happen. Would the ant live? Would he die? But the end of the book left us with "I'll leave the boy with the held up shoe. Now what do you think that boy should do?"

Silence.

The students did not know what to say. But within seconds, they had lots to say, and the room erupted with strong opinions about this particular boy, this particular ant, and killing teeny animals in general. Had the boy put his foot down on the ant or had he walked away, our discussion would have been more subdued. Those Hooses left a question in the air, and it stirred us up.

In a brief article by Elizabeth Preston in *Ask* titled "A Fish with an Eye for Faces" (2016), we learn that archer fish are able to identify human faces when rewarded with treats. The article ends, however, with a question hanging in the air: "The fish chose the right face almost every time. Since fish have much simpler brains than people do, though, scientists aren't sure how they do it" (3). This thought is not stated as a direct question, but the article ends with uncertainty. It leaves a question in our mind.

Lesléa Newman explains that "Little Cat" was inspired by a nagging and unresolvable question from her life. Writing to answer our own nagging questions opens us up. We don't always know. It is freeing and engaging and stimulating to still ask—it is healthy to not always know. Give students opportunities to write toward their own real questions, to suggest that they may or may not find answers.

Readers respond differently to ambiguous endings. Some feel that it's better to know and not be left with questions, that the author owes them an answer. Others feel that it's good *not* to know—they enjoy the electric energy that sparks from a dangling question. Whether readers appreciate endings that leave them questioning or not, there's no doubt that they get readers thinking and talking.

TRY IT

Talk with your students about books and movies that have left them with questions. Or read a text with an unresolved ending to give students a common discussion experience, a book like Dr. Seuss' *The Lorax*. Some students might feel annoyed when an author does not wrap everything up neatly. If so, acknowledge this feeling and talk about it.

Ask students to generate their own hard-to-answer questions about

- science or social studies content

- their own lives

- current events

- issues of right and wrong

- reasons people act as they do

As with the exploration "Begin with a Question," encourage students to revisit their question lists when they're writing in any genre. Questions, answered or unanswered, are generative, and as writing teachers our work is to help students generate words, sentences, ideas they never knew they had, and a hunger to keep asking. Writers can lead with questions, yes—but they can end with them too.

Disappointment

I crept down the stairs
Peering at the tree-
Holding my breath.

When I look at all the toys-
Piled so high,
They could Practically touch the bright blue sky
And eat the white cotton candy clouds.

I creep on to the floor
Trying not to make a sand-
My brother would tattle on me if he hears me.
I tip toe towards the biggest bag that reads my
name in script.

I peer inside
to find a giant wad of tissue paper
covering the treasure

I guess I'll just have to wait and see,
what that big bag holds for me.

By: Sophie R.
Grade 3

Who is There?

The moon wakes
From a long slumber
The stars twinkle
Out in the night sky

Most everything is asleep,
Except for some
Who are out and about
In the darkness.

I hear a hum
Coming from the trees
Who is there?

I hear a coo
Coming from the trees
Who is there?

I wonder
What it could be
For all I can say is...
Who is there?

by Caroline B.
Grade 6

Pen, Not an Ordinary Object

A pen is a fragile tool,
slender, light,
sometimes elegant.
Pluma, in Spanish
feminine and singular.

But don't be mistaken
as she owns words,
treasures that outlast empires
polished like diamonds
powerful as justice
beautiful as peace
helpful
to hope
love,
rebel.

—*F. Isabel Campoy*

WORDS FROM THE POET

I climbed the steps slowly in this springboard-poem, preparing to bounce in a triple pike into the truth of my soul. I used a funnel technique, building the juxtaposition of woman and pen with the assonance of key words. To bestow maximum power to the final word, I created a hyperbole in the second stanza and slowly tapered the final lines to end with one single word. This last word of this poem embodies its entire meaning.

CONSIDER THE TECHNIQUE

In F. Isabel Campoy's poem, the lines shorten as readers approach the ending. They taper. As we know, line breaks give readers clues about how to read poems, and long lines flow more quickly than short ones. Since line breaks signal slowing down, more breaks signal more slowing down. In this way, a poem like Campoy's winds down carefully, focusing our reading attention on the last word, which Campoy writes, "embodies its entire meaning." In the same way we concentrate sun rays with a magnifying glass onto a small point, we can light a fire with language, bringing our words to a point in the conclusion.

Writers of prose often choose to end a piece with one word or a short phrase, halting a reader's experience, breaking the rhythm of a text at its end. For example, Sudie Bond Noland closes her *This I Believe* essay, "The True Value of Life" (2011), with a one-liner. Injured for ten years after having been hit by a drunk driver, Noland reflects on her pain and also on what she has gained from her suffering, closing with a one-line paragraph directed toward the man who hit her: "For that, Eddy, I thank you." This abrupt sentence, standing as a concluding paragraph, highlights Noland's feelings and leaves a reader holding her closing few words.

In her nonfiction book *Titanic: Voices from the Disaster* (2012), Deborah Hopkinson ends chapter 7 with these two paragraphs, the second of which is brief and in its brevity foreboding.

> *But the distress signals would only work if there were other ships nearby to see—and understand—that the Titanic was in mortal danger.*
> *And that was not to be. (99)*

A longer sentence followed by a short one is striking in its meter, placing a stark emphasis on the final line.

Writing is full of music, and while punctuation has been compared to the musical notes of language, so too are the lengths of our phrases and sentences. Authors of varied genres know that one way to create the sound of finality is with one brief phrase or even one word. Try it. The end. Amen. Yes.

TRY IT

Show your students how poets such as Campoy create a funnel structure in a poem, tapering to a final one word or brief line. Compare this tapering to the way a dog will settle into a dog bed by turning around and around in circles and then—thunk. He's asleep. A poet can do this too—around and around and thunk—a one-liner or brief phrase ends the piece. "Listen to the way this ending flickers out slowly at the end," you might say, "like a bonfire fading away, coal by coal."

We do not always experience this funneling, however. Instead, writers of all genres may simply end abruptly, with one word or a short phrase. Encourage your students to find examples of this in your shared and their independent reading, perhaps collecting such one-word/short-phrase endings on a chart. Then have them try this technique with one of their own notebook entries. Students might choose a one-word or short-phrase ending when they want to

- make an emotional impact
- emphasize a point
- leave a thought that lingers
- shock readers

Keep this ending technique alive in your classroom as your students write in different genres.

STUDENT POEMS TO SHARE

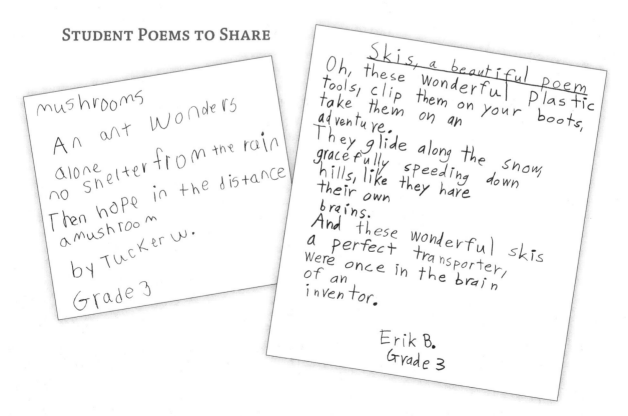

mushrooms

An ant wonders
alone
no shelter from the rain
Then hope in the distance
a mushroom
by Tucker W.
Grade 3

Skis, a beautiful poem
Oh, these wonderful plastic
tools, clip them on your boots,
take them on an
adventure.
They glide along the snow
gracefully, speeding down
hills, like they have
their own
brains.
And these wonderful skis
a perfect transporter,
were once in the brain
of an
inventor.

Erik B.
Grade 3

One Day

A parachute
with a man attached
flecked my sky
like a freckle.
I'd been counting clouds,
puff by puff,
as they drifted by
and there he was.
No plane, no drone,
no two-lane trail.
Just a tiny unexpected speck
gliding down the sky.
Gliding down the sky!
He couldn't see me from so far,
couldn't hear the
oof! of breath
his freedom squeezed from me.
He landed in a field somewhere
too far from my square of grass
to ask how it is to fly
how it is to be air
how it is to breathe
how it is to be free from a square of grass
how it is

—*Renée M. LaTulippe*

WORDS FROM THE POET

When I was a girl growing up in a small town, I used to watch planes pass overhead and wonder where all the people were going, and I'd wish I could go somewhere too. I also used to watch my father skydive and always thought it must be so freeing to fly like that! I tried to express those inner wishes for freedom in the poem "One Day," in which the narrator's imagination is captured by the sudden appearance of a skydiver, but her constraints of age and place (the square of grass) make it impossible for her to get closer to the freedom she desires. Ending poems with an inner reflection—a wish, a hope, or a thought—is a good way to leave your readers with something to think about or make them reflect on their own experiences.

CONSIDER THE TECHNIQUE

In the last few lines of "One Day," Renée M. LaTulippe's speaker steps out of her "square of grass" and into her heart, imagining the feeling of flight and freedom. By doing so, LaTulippe leaves readers with their own questions about "how it is" to be free and flying like the skydiver she once observed. LaTulippe's trip inward takes readers inward too.

As teachers, we often talk with students about balancing the "inside story" of a character with the "outside story." We remind them to not only tell what happened but describe and show how it made a character think and feel. Readers are curious to peek into the motivations and questions and emotions of speakers both real and imagined, and one way to end a text is to go inward. Writers frequently close a piece of writing by sharing a thought or reflecting upon an experience, offering a hope or a regret. Such endings may feel friendly or dreamy or even confessional.

We find this type of ending mostly in narrative or opinion pieces in which the speaker is present in the writing. In her *Orion Magazine* essay "Recovery Season" (2015), Michelle Robertson closes with this reflection about her relationship with her dad and with nature: "As soon as our eyes met, he looked away, but in that brief glance, I knew what he was telling me. I needed to trust my instincts. I needed to get back into the pond."

TRY IT

Students often write easily about actions but forget to include reactions. You might give students typed texts of articles or picture books, asking them to note and highlight where and when an author plunges inward. Pay particular attention to endings that draw on internal thinking, hopes, and reflections.

Teach students specific words and phrases that signal thinking and feeling, as Nancie Atwell does in a wonderful lesson from *Lessons That Change Writers* (2002). In Lesson 20, Atwell offers students a list of phrases, including

- He/She/I thought about _____ .

- He/She/I wondered if _____ .

- He/She/I hated it when _____ .

- He/She/I loved it when _____ .

- He/She/I couldn't believe _____ .

- He/She/I remembered _____ .

- He/She/I imagined _____ .

- He/She/I hoped _____ .

Invite students to experiment with these sentence stems to explore their topics and possible conclusions. Encourage them to revisit notebook entries, jotting answers to these questions in the margins. Students can use their marginal notes to write a few possible endings to an entry or a draft, focusing on inner thoughts and feelings.

Like Father, Like Son

A long time ago
... about 4 years
A great man
known as my father,
got cancer
When I was only two
On October 22, 2007
he unfortunately died
I am going to follow
his footsteps
Like father,
Like Son
Every single day
I wish
For him to come back

by Richard R.
grade 6

(PanaRican is a mix of my culture because I'm PuertoRican and Panamanian)

PanaRican Food

Fresh cooked food
The smell of emparadas,
Coming from the kitchen.
Made from scratch
freshly baked
Everything smells deliciously great.
Passed down
From generation
To generation
All the foods have a great taste of sensation.
Pan Dulce,
Arroz amarillo,
My Puertorican Mama makes the best food
Ojaldas frying in the kitchen,
Tostones smashed by hand.
Flan my favorite dessert.
Sweet like carmel and soft like a pillow
Seafood ceviche raw but marinated with lime so good.
Sancocho perfect for chilly days.
My Panamanian Grandma Jackie makes the best food.
Out of all these foods PanaRican food is the best.
It's better than the rest
It's apart of my culture it's apart of me.
And I'm so happy to be PanaRican.

By Natalia R.
Grade 7

(PanaRican es una mezcla de mi cultura porque soy Puertorriqueña y Panameña)

Comida PanaRican

Comida fresca cocinada
El olor a empanadas,
Viniendo de la cocina.
Hecha desde cero
Recién horneado
Todo huele deliciosamente bien.
Transmitidos
De generación
En generación
Todos los alimentos tienen un gran sabor de la sensación.
Pan Dulce,
Arroz amarillo,
Mi Mama Puertorriqueña hace la mejor comida.
Ojaldas freír en la conica,
Tostones destrozados a mano.
Flan mi postre favorito
Dulce como el caramelo y suave como una almohada
Ceviche de mariscos crudo pero marinado con limon tan buena
Sancocho perfecto para los días fríos.
Mi Panameña abuela Jackie hace la mejor comida.
De todos estos alimentos la comida PanaRican es la mejor.
Es mejor que el resto.
Y estoy tan feliz de ser PanaRican

By Natalia R., grade 7

Putting in the Work

Pop hurt his ankle while helping build
a new house on the other end of town.
"I twisted it, I guess," he said. It took all
my strength to get his work boot off.
Pop's ankle was the color of nightfall,
his foot had ballooned to twice its size.
When Mom said, "Honey, please go to the hospital."
He whispered, "We don't have insurance."

Few hours later he woke up, muttered,
"Time to go to my next job." Me and Mom
helped him put on his boot, afterwards
we were all covered in so much sweat
it looked like we'd come out of a rainstorm.
Mom pleaded, "Honey, take the night off, please?"
He shook his head. "Money doesn't fall
from the sky, you go out there and earn it."

Every time my friends ask me why I
never complain about anything . . .
I don't say a word.

—*Charles Waters*

© 2018 by Amy Ludwig VanDerwater, from *Poems Are Teachers*. Portsmouth, NH: Heinemann

WORDS FROM THE POET

I read a story about how former professional basketball player Larry Bird's father, Joe, had a swollen ankle and how young Larry had to help him take off his boot after work and put on his boot before work, how ugly and swollen his ankle was, and how his father never complained. When Larry experienced injuries in the latter stages of his career, people marveled about how he never complained.

When I write endings I often think about sticking the landing. Leaving readers with something to carry with them, in this case, how a parent's work ethic or dignity is carried onto another generation. How the end of this poem is a new beginning for the son/daughter of the story. I've found that sometimes endings are actually new beginnings for something lovely to happen in one's life.

CONSIDER THE TECHNIQUE

Writers hope to change readers, in ways big and small. Sometimes we change our readers by giving them a laugh; sometimes we open up their hearts or make them wonder. Sometimes writers leave readers with a message.

We find obvious messages at the end of any one of Aesop's fables. For example, "The Flatterer lives at the expense of those who will listen to him," from "The Fox and the Crow" (2017). Fables whack us over the head with their morals, and the message after a fable usually stands alone, right at the end.

In his poem "Putting in the Work," Charles Waters chooses to close with the imagined thoughts of the speaker child. He is more subtle than Aesop, but his meaning is clear: "Don't complain. Life is much worse for others than it is for you." Unlike Aesop, Waters lets readers figure out his message for themselves.

Students will be familiar with books that end with a message. Jacqueline Woodson's picture book *Each Kindness* (2012), about Chloe, who is repeatedly unkind to a classmate, closes with "I watched the water ripple as the sun set through the maples and the chance of a kindness with Maya became more and more forever gone." While Chloe is not telling us what to think, we read her words and reflect on our own lives: "Be kind when you can" or "You don't always get a second chance."

In persuasive writing and other types of nonfiction, writers often hand off a message at the end, sometimes as a warning, sometimes as a beacon. In his

This I Believe essay, "Failure Is a Good Thing" (2006), Jon Carroll closes with this message to his granddaughter—and to readers:

> *I probably won't tell her that failure is a good thing, because that's not a lesson you can learn when you're five. I hope I can tell her, though, that it's not the end of the world. Indeed, with luck, it is the beginning.*

By signing off with a message, writers leave readers holding a handful of hopefully life-changing words—much like the final words I speak to my children whenever they leave: "Have fun. Be safe. I love you." As a mom, I ask myself, "What message do I want my children to remember?" As writers, before we close, we ask a similar question: "What message do I want my readers to remember?"

TRY IT

Considering this ending technique may beget a slew of new writing ideas, and this itself is a gift. Invite your students to list some beliefs they hold dear. Or have them answer any of these questions:

- What have I learned from others?
- What have I learned on my own?
- What matters to me?
- What message can I offer the world?

Show students how you might draft a notebook entry with a message ending in mind, writing toward it, asking of each section, "Does this paragraph move me toward my final message?"

Another way to play with this ending technique is to read a finished draft or notebook entry in any genre, asking, "Is there a message or big idea here? What message do I want to leave for my readers?" Have students write in the margins of old entries, jotting the lessons they have learned from their own lives, lessons they might pass on through writing. Then ask them to try closing their pieces with these messages, subtly . . . or not.

The Beach

This is the beach.
Waves crashing.
People laughing.
With the icecream man just sitting
there. I even see someone-
littering out of the conner
of my eye. I see a seagull
trying to eat a bottle.
I say to myself, this stuff-
there can't be at the beach.
The animals will be in trouble.
If they eat this stuff.
Our stuff
They will be in trouble.

We need you to stop littering.
We need to start caring.

By. Bryce P.
grade 3

"Try Harder"

The black and white
soccer ball sat on
the soccer field.
The young boy shot
The soccer ball.
But he didn't make it in
The goal.
So he tried harder and harder.
He kicked it again and he scored.

In soccer you can never stop
Trying.
You have to run up and
Down the field and when you are
Close enough, you shoot.

This is not just a lesson for soccer
But for life

By: Dylan K.
Third grade

6

WRITERS SELECT TITLES

While students may believe they must title their books, articles, and poems before writing them, the truth is that quite often authors do not title their works until they have finished drafting and revising. Some parents do not name a baby until after they have studied its features and personality; they then choose a name that feels like a perfect match. Similarly, writers do not always name their book-children before they are fully born and developed.

Often, young writers simply stick labels on their stories or books. Think: "My Cat," "My Grandpa," "Our Beach Trip," "How to Play Baseball." And sometimes a label works well. Sometimes it's perfect. But titles can also help readers understand the viewpoint of an author, offer clues about what to expect, or make readers curious about the words to follow. Some titles name people, some name places, and some speak directly to readers. Some titles are mysterious, and some are alliterative. A title can make a person feel sad, include a pun, or incite anger. Writers think about many possibilities when they choose titles. In a way, a title is a peek into the future.

A writer considers many things when crafting a title. When I title a poem, I ask myself if I wish to create a bit of mystery or to let readers know right away what to expect. I reread the poem to see if one line encapsulates what matters most, and if so, I repeat this line in the title spot. I consider freshness in a title, asking, "Is this too common a phrase?" I also strive to write titles that feel friendly to readers, and even when writing about a controversial topic, I aim not to offend readers before they even make it to the first line. Other writers choose differently, but all of us know that titles matter. Readers do judge texts based on titles, and this judgment determines whether they read on.

Professional authors do not always have the opportunity to select their own titles, however. Rather, titles are frequently written by editors or by a marketing team. Newspapers, magazines, and books are sold for money, and websites depend on clicks, so titling is often a marketing decision as much as anything else. Never once has a column I've written for the *Buffalo News* kept the title I submitted. In fact, a column written by the same author may be titled differently in different newspapers, as is the case with the February 2017 article by Leonard Pitts beginning with the line, "White terrorism is not as bad as Muslim terrorism." Which of the following titles would be most likely to keep you reading?

"If the Mass Shooter Is White, Well, Is That Really So Bad?"
—*Miami Herald*

"Double Standard on White Terrorism"—*St. Louis Post-Dispatch*

"White Terrorism Not as Bad as Muslim Terrorism?"—*USA Today*

When we teach our students to write and publish their own pieces, we should set time aside for them to experiment with different titles, drafting many possibilities and talking together about which works best and why.

Learn to Select Titles from Poems

A poet may leave a poem untitled, but most poems have names, just as people do, and writers can study titles to learn new title possibilities. Take a look at some of the titles of poems in this book, listed below. How would you categorize them? What can students learn about titling from a random list like this one?

"The Longest Home Run"

"Night"

"Miracle in the Collection Plate"

"Yes, Boys Can Dance!"

"Putting in the Work"

"Go Away, Cat"

"a dream is like"

"Mary Todd Lincoln Speaks of Her Son's Death, 1862"

"Pelican"

"Poem for a Bully"

By simply thinking about this list, you know that titles may answer yet-to-be-asked questions or name the speaker. Titles may describe a time of day or name the person addressed. Titles might give a direction or introduce a speaker and setting. Making lists of titles and talking about them, sorting them in much the same way you might sort buttons (plastic, metal, glass), helps students understand that no matter what they are writing, they can use the same strategies to grow their title banks. Studying a list of titles in any genre is the best way for students to imagine possibilities for titling their own works.

This chapter highlights three possible titling techniques that can be used as a springboard for discovering other possibilities. Strangely, surprisingly, and enchantingly, each title is about doors.

One Blue Door

To make a poem
listen: crow calls.
Rain paints a door,
blue in the sky.

To make a poem
you need the door
blue and lonely
swinging in the rain.

To make a poem
you need to leap
through that blue door
onto a crow.

To make a poem
you need to glide
on crow's black *caw*,
skimming the trees.

To make a poem
you need to taste
petals of rain.
Open your mouth.

To make a poem
you need to hear
fountains sprouting
in your hands.

Leap through one blue door
onto crow's black call.
Catch rain's petal-fall.
Music in your hands.

Leap through one blue door.

—*Pat Mora*

WORDS FROM THE POET

I am a reader and a reviser. I hope these make me a better cook, gardener, parent, advocate, and writer. I explore. To title these lines, "to make a poem," a phrase repeated six times in this poem, was a possibility, but felt flat, though I liked the making idea. There is something a bit mysterious about "one blue door." The three words, and the memory of the Santa Fe door, snagged me. I hope they snag you.

CONSIDER THE TECHNIQUE

The title for Pat Mora's poem "One Blue Door" comes from three words repeated together twice near the end of her poem. Sometimes a writer chooses a line for the title straight from the text, and it's not always the line that's most obvious. Mora could have chosen the line repeated throughout the text—"to make a poem"—but as she reflects, it felt flat. She went for mystery instead, and a line that snagged her.

Writers of all genres sometimes use a significant word or phrase in the text as the title. It might be a repeated line or an alliterative combination of words or simply a word or phrase that feels representative of the whole. The title for Michael Ian Black's *A Pig Parade Is a Terrible Idea* comes from a repeating line woven throughout this essay parody in picture-book form. Margaret Mitchell considered several titles for her novel *Gone with the Wind* (1936), eventually settling on a phrase that appears in the novel itself. The lines read, "Was Tara still standing? Or was Tara also gone with the wind which had swept through Georgia?"

When we title our essays and stories, our poems and books and songs and articles, we choose what readers will read—and judge—first. Often, the most fitting representation of a work of writing is a sound that echoes from within a line or a phrase of soon-to-be-read words.

TRY IT

The best way to understand any technique is to romp through strong examples, so invite your students to wallow in titles, highlighting those that spring straight from texts whole.

After title-treasure-hunting through science magazines and newspaper headlines, poems and favorite books, discuss these straight-from-text titles. Which are repeating lines? Which are found at the text's conclusion? Which spring from a lead? Which title-lines can be found in the middle of a story or an article?

Talk about why an author may have chosen one from-text title over another. Encourage your students to listen to their title possibilities as Mora does, understanding that sometimes words that work well inside a text seem to "fall flat" as a title. Writers develop their writing-ears as they go, and the more you write with intention, the more finely tuned your ears become. Sometimes a particular title just feels right, but you can only know how right it feels if you have tried on many titles of all shapes and sizes in your writing dressing room.

Teach students to play with title selection when stakes are low, when there is no audience, in notebooks. Ask them to open their notebooks to a random page, reading the entry carefully, highlighting phrases or words that might work as titles. Have students list the title possibilities atop the same notebook page or on a sticky note, then talk with partners about which titles "feel right" and which "fall flat."

Later, try this same exercise with drafts to-be-published, pressing students to go beyond their first-glance titles, to read carefully for the one word or group of words embedded in a mountain of text. Demonstrate that by rereading, writers can discover that rough emerald, just waiting to be dug free and reset as a sparkly title.

STUDENT POEMS TO SHARE

Fiery Horse

A fiery horse runs Free
and that's how it must Be
if he is kept in a stable
he will turn to ICE,
he will
he will
By Kate P.
grade 3

Someone Special

There is someone kind
Day after day, works hard,
teaches and has a warm
heart. Someone that their
heart never darkens,
Someone Special.

By: Love A.
Grade 4

When I Open the Door

My mind welcomes me, huge room—calm down, step inside.

Inside feels so much cooler than out, steaming 97 degrees.

It's like a grocery store, piled plums and peaches—

this door opens by itself, magic door, with a secret eye on me.

My memory seems long and curling, shining ribbon on a reel.

I feel lucky to live in a world of doors, downtown doors,

doors on the bus folding open, smooth sliding doors on the train,

creaky door at Grandma's, doors of every minute and day.

Who could be bored in a world of doors? Like Grandma always says,

It's up to you, baby, up to you.

Turn the knob, the handle, the latch, the key.

My notebook winks hopefully—what will you write this time?

—*Naomi Shihab Nye*

© 2018 by Amy Ludwig VanDerwater from Poems Are Teachers. Portsmouth, NH: Heinemann.

WORDS FROM THE POET

Sometimes I like to think of simple lines that could serve as "openers"—"I never knew" or "I like to remember"—and then write from there. For "When I Open the Door" the title suggests both real and imagined doors and also gives us the power. That's nice!

CONSIDER THE TECHNIQUE

When we read the title of Naomi Shihab Nye's "When I Open the Door," we are led straight into the poem itself. Nye does not repeat the words "when I open the door" in the first line of her poem. Rather, her title provides words that walk us into the garden of her text. Nye's title leads her to write more. We find this frequently in poems, and it is logical and elegant to waltz from title to first line because readers need not open covers or turn pages to get there. With a brief eye movement, we see it all on the same page.

This is a special titling technique for poetry, and it works because the form of a poem keeps title and first lines on the same page. We can teach our students to do as Nye does, to think of "simple lines that could serve as 'openers.'" In this way, titling is also a way to discover ideas.

Similarly, students seeking strong titles for their already finished pieces may decide to look at their leads, asking, "Do I begin with powerful words that might work as a title?" For example, the first line of this book's introduction echoes the title, *Poems Are Teachers*, and the book (hopefully) explains exactly how.

TRY IT

Experiment with Nye's suggestion, inviting students to write a variety of possible "openers." See which genres show up on the page. Let the titles lead you right into a text. Brainstorm some opener titles together, perhaps offering students a start with lines such as

- When I _____
- The Last Time _____
- If You _____
- Once There Was _____
- I'll Never Forget _____
- I Like to _____

By playing with titles-as-inspiration, as Nye does, your titles will be the first words you write. Try following a title into an opinion piece, a story, an informational piece. Follow where a title leads.

We can be best friends

We can ride a Roller coaster
or play some basketball
come with me

We can be best friends
come with me

Alexandra B.
Grade 5

When I told time to wait

It turned its back on me
it kept walking,
it kept running.
Life is because of time,
Joy is because of time.
You hate time like it's a horrible man,
but you love time, like it's your mother.

It doesn't stop,
and surely not for you.
Time won't look back
it won't walk backwards,
it's fragile like glass
it's strong like metal.
Time may slow down
time may speed up
but time won't stop.
It will never stop.

-Sara O.
Grade 6

The Lion at the Door

His teeth are sharp.
His jaws immense.
He's big. He's scary.
Will he let me pass?

Why does he sit
at the library door
instead of roaming
wild grasslands?

Here comes a girl
with library books.
"Bye, Lion," she says.
"See you next time."

I can't believe
how scared I was
of a library lion
made of stone.

—*Juanita Havill*

Sometimes I look for a title in a line or phrase in the poem that will catch the attention of the reader. I don't think of the title as a sign on a door telling you what is inside. Instead, the door is cracked open and a word or phrase reaches out and beckons you in. If the title can be amusing, puzzling, or mysterious, I am happy.

CONSIDER THE TECHNIQUE

While many titles offer a summary of a text or quickly name the topic or subject, some titles make a reader wonder, "What will this be about?" Finding Juanita Havill's poem "The Lion at the Door" on a contents page, you might assume that a real lion awaits, right outside the speaker's home. You might wonder, "What lion? Which door?" Because Havill doesn't give her subject away, it is only in stanza 2 that you come to realize that this title's hinted-at lion must be Patience or Fortitude, one of the well-loved marble lions standing guard at the New York Public Library at Fifth Avenue and Forty-second Street in Manhattan.

Havill writes, "I don't think of the title as a sign on a door telling you what is inside. Instead, the door is cracked open and a word or phrase reaches out and beckons you in. If the title can be amusing, puzzling, or mysterious, I am happy." Authors consider their readers, right down to title selection, asking, "How will this title affect the person who picks up my text?"

Many writers of opinion and information, narrative and poetry, enjoy teasing readers with titles that hint or titles that may even be a bit misleading. Such a setup creates a more satisfying "Aha!" later, when a reader understands the connection between title and text. For example, in the January/February 2017 issue of the *Atlantic*, I noticed three mysterious titles: "Big in Japan: Tiny Food" by Jessica Leigh Hester; "What the Octopus Knows" by Olivia Judson; and "The Ninja Cure for Anxiety" by James Parker. These titles, not revealing too much of their subjects, beckon, and when a reader is curious about a mysterious title, he is likely to read on.

Writers reveal meaning bit by bit, in much the same way that a fisherwoman lets out a few inches of line at a time, luring that fish into the boat without its even knowing what's happening. A writer need not give a subject away before line one, but instead may choose to name a book or poem with a small clue or mere suggestion at what lies beyond title or cover.

TRY IT

Invite students to look closely at books on your classroom shelves, pulling ones that feel mysterious. How does a writer craft a title that plants a question in a reader's mind? How does a writer suggest a subject? Which mysterious titles intrigue you most?

Show students how you might draft a mysterious title for one of your own notebook entries or drafts. Is there a clue you might give? A hint? Is there a way you might play with words or double meanings as Havill has done in "The Lion at the Door"? Model how to write titles that don't "give it all away," using notebooks to list potential mysterious titles.

As you explore different genres, have students share title possibilities in small groups, inviting talk about which ones most pique each reader's curiosity and why.

STUDENT POEMS TO SHARE

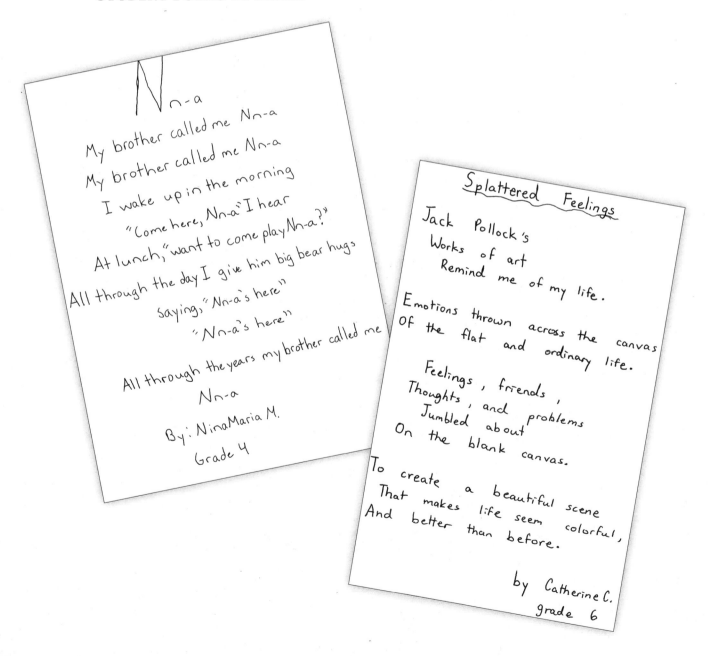

Nn-a

My brother called me Nn-a
My brother called me Nn-a
I wake up in the morning
"Come here, Nn-a" I hear
At lunch, "want to come play Nn-a?"
All through the day I give him big bear hugs
saying, "Nn-a's here"
"Nn-a's here"

All through the years my brother called me
Nn-a

By: NinaMaria M.
Grade 4

Splattered Feelings

Jack Pollock's
Works of art
Remind me of my life.

Emotions thrown across the canvas
Of the flat and ordinary life.

Feelings, friends,
Thoughts, and problems
Jumbled about
On the blank canvas.

To create a beautiful scene
That makes life seem colorful,
And better than before.

by Catherine C.
grade 6

IN CLOSING

This book celebrates poems and poets, along with various writing techniques that poetry study offers all writers. Poems teach us how to be stronger writers. But more importantly, if we let them, poems teach us how to be stronger, kinder, wiser human beings. May it be so for each of us—and for the young ones we meet and teach.

I close with the words of my teacher Lee Bennett Hopkins:

As

sun rises

as

moon sets

as

oceans roar

there
will be
more and more and more and more

poetry

here
there
wherever

more than ever before

forever

for

poetry

is

must

will

always be

—*Lee Bennett Hopkins*

A Guide to the Poets

Alma Flor Ada, professor emerita, University of San Francisco, has devoted her life to advocacy for peace and social justice. Among her many prestigious awards are the Christopher (*The Gold Coin*), Pura Belpré (*Under the Royal Palms*), Once Upon a World (*Gathering the Sun*), Parents' Choice Honor (*Dear Peter Rabbit*), NCSS Notable Book (*My Name Is María Isabel*), and International Latino Book Award (*Love Amalia; Dancing Home;* and *Yes! We Are Latinos*). She has received the Virginia Hamilton Award for her body of work and the OHTLI Award from the Mexican government for her services to Mexican communities. http://almaflorada.com

Arnold Adoff is a renowned poet and anthologist of African American literature who has published more than thirty books for young readers and their older allies, including the seminal *Black Is Brown Is Tan*, which was the first children's book to portray an interracial family. He is the recipient of the NCTE Award for Excellence in Poetry for Children for the body of his work, and his most recent collection, *Roots and Blues: A Celebration*, won the Lion and the Unicorn Prize for North American Youth Poetry. www.arnoldadoff .com and www.poetandonewomanband.com

Kwame Alexander is the *New York Times* bestselling author of twenty-one books, including *Booked* and *The Crossover*, which received the 2015 John Newbery Medal for the Most Distinguished Contribution to American Literature for Children, the Coretta Scott King Author Award Honor, the NCTE Charlotte Huck Honor, the Lee Bennett Hopkins / Penn State Poetry Award, and the Paterson Poetry Prize. Alexander's other works include *Surf's Up; Crush: Love Poems for Teenagers;* and *He Said, She Said*. Alexander believes that poetry can change the world. www.kwamealexander.com

Jeannine Atkins writes about strong girls and women. Her books of verse include *Finding Wonders: Three Girls Who Changed Science; Borrowed Names: Poems About Laura Ingalls Wilder, Madam C. J. Walker, Marie Curie, and Their Daughters;* and *Stone Mirrors: The Sculpture and Silence of Edmonia Lewis*. www.Jeannine Atkins.com

Doraine Bennett writes poetry and nonfiction for children. She lives with her husband in Georgia, where she watches herons in her backyard creek. She enjoys blowing bubbles, practicing yoga, and playing with her grandchildren. www.dorainebennett.com

Robyn Hood Black makes poems and art in the South Carolina Lowcountry, where sea breezes beckon and Spanish moss ghosts the live oaks. Her poetry appears in several anthologies for young readers and in leading haiku journals. She makes vintage found-poem art, among other things, through her Etsy business, artsyletters. www.robynhoodblack.com

Susan Blackaby dabbles across genres in both educational and trade publishing. Her many titles include *Brownie Groundhog and the February Fox*; *The Twelve Days of Christmas in Oregon*; and an award-winning poetry collection, *Nest, Nook, and Cranny*. She lives along the bluffs and banks of the Pacific Northwest. www.susanblackaby.com

F. Isabel Campoy is the award-winning author of more than one hundred children's books. She is a recognized scholar devoted to promoting diverse books in diverse languages. She is the recipient of the 2016 Ramón Santiago Award, among others, and a member of the North American Academy of the Spanish Language. www.isabelcampoy.com

Deborah Chandra has written several children's books, among them *Rich Lizard*; *A Is for Amos*; and *George Washington's Teeth*, written with Madeleine Comora. She was awarded the International Reading Association / Lee Bennett Hopkins Poetry Award. Chandra lives in Southern California, where she has taught second and third graders, whom she describes as playful, frankly sensual, and very much a part of their surroundings.

Kate Coombs has published seven children's books, including the award-winning poetry collection *Water Sings Blue*. Her most recent book of poems is called *Breathe and Be*. She has also written middle grade fiction and picture books, including *The Tooth Fairy Wars*. Coombs lives in Utah, where she listens for the trash truck every Monday morning. www.katecoombs.com

Kristy Dempsey works as a teacher and librarian in Belo Horizonte, Brazil, where the rhythms of samba have danced their way into her writing. She is the author of *A Dance Like Starlight*, a JLG selection, ALA Notable Book, Bank Street Best of 2015, CCBC Choice, and winner of the 2015 Golden Kite Award for Picture Book Text, as well as many other picture books. www.kristydempsey.com

Rebecca Kai Dotlich grew up in the Midwest, spending her days ice skating, exploring trails by the creek, reading comic books, and cutting out paper dolls. Her books have been awarded a Boston Globe Horn Book Honor, a Golden Kite Picture Book Honor, and a Bank Street Best Book of the Year. She was an SB&F Subaru Prize finalist for excellence in science books. Dotlich's work appears in dozens of anthologies, magazines, and textbooks. She lives in Indiana and has four grandchildren, who help her eat homemade cookies and macaroni and cheese. www.rebeccakaidotlich.com

David Elliott is the award-winning author of more than twenty picture books and novels for young people, including *Bull*, a YA retelling-in-verse of the myth of Theseus and the Minotaur, and *Baabwaa and Wooliam*, a picture book illustrated by Melissa Sweet in which two sheep share an adventure in their own backyard. Elliott lives in New Hampshire with his wife and their Dandie Dinmont terrier, Queequeg. www.davidelliottbooks.com

Margarita Engle is the 2017–2019 Young People's Poet Laureate, selected by The Poetry Foundation. She is the Cuban-America author of verse novels such as the Newbery Honor book, *The Surrender Tree*, and the PEN USA Award winner, *The Lightning Dreamer*. Her verse memoir, *Enchanted Air*, received a Pura Belpré Medal, Golden Kite Award, Lee Bennett Hopkins / Penn State Poetry Award, and Arnold Adoff Multicultural Poetry Award, among others. *Drum Dream Girl* received a Charlotte Zolotow Award for best picture-book text. Margarita lives in central California. www.margaritaengle.com

Matt Forrest Esenwine is author of *Flashlight Night* and coauthor of *Don't Ask a Dinosaur* (2018). His children's poetry can be found in numerous anthologies, including *Lullaby and Kisses Sweet*, the *National Geographic Book of Nature Poetry*, and The Poetry Friday Anthology series. www.mattforrest.com

Douglas Florian has written and illustrated more than fifty books for children. These include *Beast Feast*, winner of the Lee Bennett Hopkins / Penn State Poetry Award; *Bow Wow Meow Meow*, winner of the Gryphon Award; *Insectlopedia*, a national bestseller; *Dinothesaurus*, a Bank Street College "Best Book of the Year"; and *Mammalabilia*, winner of the Claudia Lewis Award for Poetry. He has presented his books of poetry at the White House, Carnegie Hall, the Museum of Modern Art in New York, and hundreds of schools across America. http://floriancafe.blogspot.com/

Kristine O'Connell George has earned honors including the Lee Bennett Hopkins / Penn State Poetry Award, the International Literacy Association / Lee Bennett Hopkins Promising Poet Award, the Golden Kite, the Claudia Lewis Poetry Award, ALA Notables, NCTE Notables, School Library Journal Best Books, and Hornbook Fanfare. A frequent speaker at schools and conferences, she is also a passionate organic gardener, hiker, and photographer. www.kristinegeorge.com

Charles Ghigna, otherwise known as Father Goose, lives in a treehouse in the middle of Alabama. He is the author of more than one hundred books and more than five thousand poems, many of which appear in textbooks, anthologies, newspapers, and magazines, from the *New Yorker* and *Harper's* to *Cricket* and *Highlights*. He served as poet-in-residence and chair of creative writing at the Alabama School of Fine Arts and as a nationally syndicated feature writer for Tribune Media Services. www.FatherGoose.com

Nikki Grimes is a *New York Times* bestselling author and the recipient of the 2017 Laura Ingalls Wilder Medal, the 2016 Virginia Hamilton Literary Award, and the 2006 NCTE Award for Excellence in Poetry for Children. Her distinguished works include the much-honored books *Garvey's Choice*; ALA Notable book *What Is Goodbye?*; Coretta Scott King Award winner *Bronx Masquerade*; and Coretta Scott King Author Honor books *Jazmin's Notebook*, *Talkin' About Bessie*, *Dark Sons*, *Words with Wings*, and *The Road to Paris*. Creator of the popular *Meet Danitra Brown*, Grimes lives in Corona, California. www.nikkigrimes.com

Mary Lee Hahn is a teacher-poet. She has taught fourth and fifth grades for thirty-plus years and is the author of *Reconsidering Read-Aloud*. She has poems in *Dear Tomato: An International Crop of Food and Agriculture Poems*, The Poetry Friday Anthology series, the *National Geographic Book of Nature Poetry*, and *The Best of Today's Little Ditty*. Hahn blogs about children's literature and teaching at A Year of Reading with Franki Sibberson, and collects her poetry online at Poetrepository. www.maryleehahn.com

David L. Harrison has written ninety-two books for children and young people. His work has received dozens of honors, been translated into numerous languages, and been anthologized more than 185 times. Harrison is regularly featured at hundreds of conferences, workshops, literature festivals, schools, and colleges across America and holds two science degrees and two honorary doctorates of letters. He has received the Pioneer in Education Award and the Missouri Library Association's Literacy Award. He is Drury University's poet laureate, and David Harrison Elementary School in Springfield, Missouri, is named in his honor. www.davidharrison.com

Juanita Havill is author of *Jamaica's Find*, several other Jamaica books, and *Grow: A Novel in Verse*. She has been writing children's books for over thirty years and believes that writing and reading poetry make us more aware and that awareness helps us understand others and the world around us. She believes that poetry is a way to celebrate life and make our hearts sing.

Georgia Heard has published numerous poems, children's books, anthologies, and books on writing, including her most recent, *Heart Maps: Helping Students Create and Craft Authentic Writing*. Her newest book for children is *Boom! Bellow! Bleat! Animal Poems for Two or More Voices* (forthcoming, 2019). Currently, she visits schools in the United States and around the world teaching writing and poetry. Heard lives in South Florida, a mile from the roar of the ocean, and enjoys long walks on the beach with her family and dog. www .georgiaheard.com

Sara Holbrook is the author of over a dozen poetry books for children, teens, and adults. Her newest book is a middle grade historical novel, *The Enemy*. Along with coauthor Michael Salinger, she is also the author of four professional books for teachers on poetry, vocabulary instruction, and performance. www.outspokenlit.com, www.saraholbrook.com

Lee Bennett Hopkins has written and edited numerous award-winning books for children and young adults. He has received the University of Southern Mississippi Medallion, the National Council of Teachers of English Award for Excellence in Poetry for Children, and the Christopher and Regina Medals. To encourage the recognition of poetry, he has established three major poetry awards: the Lee Bennett Hopkins / Penn State Poetry Award, the International Literacy Association / Lee Bennett Hopkins Promising Poet Award, and the Lee Bennett Hopkins Society of Children's Book Writers and Illustrators Poetry Award. He was recently inducted into the Florida Artists Hall of Fame. www.leebennetthopkins.com

Paul B. Janeczko is a writer of poetry and nonfiction, as well as a noted anthologist. His award-winning poetry anthologies include *A Poke in the I; A Kick*

in the Head; *A Foot in the Mouth*; and *Firefly July*. He is the author of *Worlds Afire*; *Requiem: Poems of the Terezín Ghetto*; *Top Secret: A Handbook of Codes, Ciphers, and Secret Writing*; *The Dark Game: True Spy Stories*; and *Double Cross: Deception Techniques in War*. Janeczko lives in midcoast Maine. www.paulbjaneczko.com

Irene Latham first wrote love poems—for her mother. An award-winning author of two novels for children, *Leaving Gee's Bend* and *Don't Feed the Boy*, and three poetry picture books, she was named the winner of the 2016 International Literary Association / Lee Bennett Hopkins Promising Poet Award. Her latest book, cowritten with Charles Waters, is *Can I Touch Your Hair? Poems of Race, Mistakes, and Friendship* (2018). www.irenelatham.com

Renée M. LaTulippe has coauthored nine early readers and a collection of poetry and has published poems in several anthologies, including the *National Geographic Book of Nature Poetry, One Minute till Bedtime*, and three editions of *The Poetry Friday Anthology*. LaTulippe teaches the online course The Lyrical Language Lab and writes a blog about children's poetry. www.nowater river.com

J. Patrick Lewis has published one hundred children's picture/poetry books to date with Creative Editions; Knopf; Atheneum; Dial; Harcourt; Little, Brown; National Geographic; Chronicle Books; Scholastic; Candlewick; and others. He received the 2010–2011 NCTE Award for Excellence in Poetry for Children, and was the Poetry Foundation's third Children's Poet Laureate of the U.S. (2011–2013). He has visited over 540 schools and libraries around the world. www.jpatricklewis.com

George Ella Lyon has written many books, the most recent of which are *Many-Storied House: Poems; Boats Float!*, cowritten with her son Benn; and *Voices from the March on Washington*, cowritten with J. Patrick Lewis. The author of "Where I'm From," Lyon served as Kentucky's poet laureate (2015–2016). www.georgeellalyon.com

Guadalupe Garcia McCall is the author of *Under the Mesquite* (a novel in verse), *Summer of the Mariposas*, and *Shame the Stars*. She lives with her husband, Jim, and their pets, Baxter, Blanca, and Luna, in the Texas countryside, where she writes poetry and is close to nature every day. www.guadalupe garciamccall.com

Pat Mora has published forty-five books for adults, teens, and children. Her children's books include editions in bilingual formats and Spanish editions.

Mora is a literacy advocate, and in 1996 she founded Children's Day, Book Day / El día de los niños / El día de los libros, often known as Día, an April 30 and yearlong initiative celebrating all children and connecting them with "bookjoy." Annually, across the country, April book fiestas strengthen communities, often on or near April 30. Mora, who has three children and one granddaughter, holds two honorary doctorates and is an honorary member of the American Library Association. www.patmora.org

Heidi Mordhorst is a full-time public school teacher and poet living in Bethesda, Maryland. Her work includes *Squeeze: Poems from a Juicy Universe* and *Pumpkin Butterfly: Poems from the Other Side of Nature*, as well as poems in numerous anthologies. She gets poetry ideas from listening to kids, from watching the world, and from typographical errors. www.myjuicylittle universe.blogspot.com

Marilyn Nelson, a three-time finalist for the National Book Award and 2016 winner of the NCTE Award for Excellence in Poetry for Children, is one of America's most celebrated poets. She is the author or translator of seventeen poetry books for adults and children and five chapbooks, and in 2014 she published a memoir, named one of NPR's Best Books of 2014, titled *How I Discovered Poetry*—a series of fifty poems about growing up in the 1950s in a military family, each poem stamped with a place and date from the many places they lived. http://marilyn-nelson.com

Kenn Nesbitt has written many books of verse for children and has long been a vocal advocate for bringing the joy of poetry into a daily routine. He served as the Poetry Foundation's Children's Poet Laureate from 2013 to 2015 and lives in a big old house in Spokane, Washington, with his family. www .poetry4kids.com

Lesléa Newman is the author of several picture books written in verse, including *Just Like Mama; Cats, Cats, Cats!*; and *Here Is the World: A Year of Jewish Holidays*, and the teen novel-in-verse *October Mourning: A Song for Matthew Shepard*. From 2008 to 2010 she served as the poet laureate of Northampton, Massachusetts. www.lesleakids.com

Naomi Shihab Nye just found the first poem she ever wrote, written at age six and called "Chicago"—with thumbtack holes in the corners (her first-grade teacher let her hang it on the hall bulletin board in Ferguson, Missouri). Nye had completely forgotten that the poem was illustrated—she had drawn tall buildings at the bottom and top of the page. She only remembered the words. http://barclayagency.com/site/speaker/naomi-shihab-nye

Ann Whitford Paul writes picture books; children's fiction, nonfiction, and poetry; and early readers and has also written a book for adults, *Writing Picture Books: A Hands-On Guide from Story Creation to Publication*. Paul has written a picture book, *Word Builder*, about writing, and a rhymed picture book titled *If Animals Said I Love You*. www.annwhitfordpaul.net

Jack Prelutsky is best known for his humorous and imaginative verse and has been making words rhyme for fifty years. His first book, *A Gopher in the Garden*, was published in 1967. A prolific poet and anthologist, Prelutsky was designated by the Poetry Foundation in 2006 as its first Children's Poet Laureate. www.jackprelutsky.com

Heidi Bee Roemer has sold nearly four hundred poems to children's magazines and anthologies. Her books include *Come to My Party and Other Shape Poems*; *What Kinds of Seeds Are These?*; *Whose Nest Is This?*; and *Peekity Boo! What Baby Can Do!* www.heidibroemer.com

Michael J. Rosen is the author, editor, illustrator, or photographer of more than 125 books for both adults and children. They range from short-story collections to poetry, from cookbooks to humor anthologies, from picture books to philanthropic anthologies. His recent books include *The Tale of Rescue*, a middle grade novel chosen as one of *Kirkus Reviews*' and the New York Public Library's best books of 2015; *Running with Trains: A Novel in Poetry and Two Voices*; and three volumes of haiku about cats, dogs, and birds, which received a trifecta of stars from *Kirkus Reviews*. www.michaeljrosen.com

Laura Purdie Salas is a former teacher and has written more than 125 books for kids, including the Can Be . . . series (Bank Street Best Books, IRA Teachers' Choice) and *BookSpeak!* (Minnesota Book Award, NCTE Notable). Salas loves visiting with educators and sharing inspiration and practical tips about poetry, nonfiction, and more through her blog, newsletter, and presentations. www.laurasalas.com

Michael Salinger is a father, poet, and educator whose life goal is to keep poetry relevant and in the classroom around the world. He has written books of poetry for all ages and has written several professional books with his coauthor and partner in rhyme, Sara Holbrook. He loves bicycling. www .outspokenlit.com

Laura Shovan is an award-winning poet, editor, and middle grade author. She conducts poetry workshops for children and teens as a longtime artist-in-residence for the Maryland State Arts Council. Her debut verse novel for children is *The Last Fifth Grade of Emerson Elementary*. www.laurashovan.com

Joyce Sidman received a Newbery Honor for her book *Dark Emperor and Other Poems of the Night* and the NCTE Award for Excellence in Poetry for Children for her award-winning body of work. She lives in Wayzata, Minnesota, where she roams the woods and meadows with her dog, Watson. www.joycesidman.com

Marilyn Singer is winner of the 2015 NCTE Award for Excellence in Poetry for Children and is the author of more than one hundred books, many of which are poetry collections, including *Miss Muffet, or What Came After* and three books of "reversos": *Mirror Mirror*; *Follow Follow*; and *Echo Echo*. Singer cohosts the Poetry Blast, which features children's poets reading their work at various conferences. She and her husband, Steve Aronson, live in Brooklyn, New York, and Washington, Connecticut, with many pets. www.marilynsinger.net

Eileen Spinelli fell in love with words and books when she was six years old. As a sophomore in high school, she won her first writing contest. With the fifty-dollar prize, she bought a typewriter and a pair of red shoes. She is married to fellow author, Jerry Spinelli, and when they are not writing, they like to hang out with their grandkids, play Scrabble, and watch old movies. www.eileenspinelli.com

Susan Marie Swanson writes for children—and with them too. She has worked in literary arts programs sponsored by COMPAS, the American Swedish Institute, the Loft Literary Center, and others. Her poem "Trouble, Fly" has appeared in a choral setting for treble voices and in an art installation in a children's hospital. One of her picture books, *The House in the Night*, won the Minnesota Book Award and the Caldecott Medal.

Amy Ludwig VanDerwater is author of *Forest Has a Song, Every Day Birds, Read! Read! Read!,* and the forthcoming *With My Hands* (2018) and *Dreaming of You* (2018). Amy authored this book, coauthored *Poetry: Big Thoughts in Small Packages*, teaches writing, and blogs for children at *The Poem Farm* and *Sharing Our Notebooks*. You can find her in Holland, New York. www.amyludwigvanderwater.com

Lee Wardlaw has written thirty books for children, including *Won Ton—A Cat Tale Told in Haiku* and *Won Ton and Chopstick*. She is the recipient of both the Lee Bennett Hopkins / Penn State Poetry Award and the Myra Cohn Livingston Award for Poetry. Wardlaw's books have also been honored by the NCTE, ALSC, CCBC, and more. www.leewardlaw.com

Charles Waters is a children's poet, actor, and educator who has performed in schools and universities across the country. His work has appeared in various textbooks and anthologies, including *Amazing Places*, the *National Geographic Book of Animal Poetry*, and The Poetry Friday Anthology series. His first book, cowritten with Irene Latham, is titled *Can I Touch Your Hair? Poems of Race, Mistakes, and Friendship* (2018). www.charleswaterspoetry.com

April Halprin Wayland writes children's books and poetry, teaches UCLA students how to write, plays the fiddle, hikes with her dog, and helps people vote. She lives with her husband, their licky, lanky dog named Eli, a tortoise named Sheldon (because he has a shell), and a cat named Snot (her husband named the cat). www.AprilWayland.com

Carole Boston Weatherford has written more than three dozen books, including *Moses: When Harriet Tubman Led Her People to Freedom*; *Gordon Parks: How the Photographer Captured Black and White America*; *Voice of Freedom: Fannie Lou Hamer, Spirit of the Civil Rights Movement*; *Becoming Billie Holiday*; and *Birmingham, 1963*. Her books have garnered many honors, including the Caldecott Honor, Coretta Scott King Award, and NAACP Image Award. She teaches at Fayetteville State University in North Carolina. www.cbweatherford.com

Steven Withrow is a poet, writer, and teacher from Falmouth, Massachusetts. He is the author of the children's poetry collection *It's Not My Fault*. His poems for children, teens, and adults appear in dozens of journals and anthologies, including the *National Geographic Book of Nature Poetry*. www.cracklesofspeech.blogspot.com

Allan Wolf is an author and performance poet living in Asheville, North Carolina. He is a two-time winner of the North Carolina YA Book Award, and his poetry has appeared in many diverse publications, from *Ladybug* magazine to the *North Carolina Literary Review*. Wolf's many books for children and teens showcase his love of history, research, and poetry. www.allanwolf.com

Janet Wong is a former lawyer who switched careers and became a children's poet. She has been featured on *The Oprah Winfrey Show* and has performed at the White House. Author of thirty children's books on writing, dumpster diving, diversity, chess, and more, Wong is a frequent speaker at schools and conferences. Her current work focuses on The Poetry Friday Anthology series. www.janetwong.com

Jane Yolen is the author of over 350 books, many of them about nature and birds—books like *Owl Moon*; *You Nest Here with Me*; *On Bird Hill*; *The Stranded Whale*; *Fine Feathered Friends*; *Bug Off!*; *Birds of a Feather*; and *An Egret's Day*. www.janeyolen.com

REFERENCES

Aesop. 2017. "The Fox and the Crow." *The Aesop for Children*. Accessed February 24. www.read.gov/aesop/027.html.

Alexander, Kwame, and Chris Colderley. 2015. "List Poetry and the Art of Classroom Storytelling." *edu@scholastic* (blog), November 24. http://edublog.scholastic.com/post/list-poetry-and-art-classroom-storytelling.

Anderson, Carl. 2000. *How's It Going?* Portsmouth, NH: Heinemann.

———. 2005. *Assessing Writers*. Portsmouth, NH: Heinemann.

Applegate, Katherine. 2014. *Ivan: The Remarkable True Story of the Shopping Mall Gorilla*. Illustrated by G. Brian Karas. New York: Clarion Books.

Atwell, Nancie. 2002. *Lessons That Change Writers*. Portsmouth, NH: Heinemann.

Bailey, Elisabeth Tova. 2010. *The Sound of a Wild Snail Eating*. Chapel Hill, NC: Algonquin Books.

Bendrick, Lou. 2010. "Gardening Through the Seasons." *Mother Nature Network* (online), June 17. www.mnn.com/your-home/organic-farming-gardening/stories/gardening-through-the-seasons.

Bingham, Molly. 2009. "Serving and Saving Humanity." *This I Believe*, November 18. http://thisibelieve.org/essay/72989/.

Bos, Carole. 2016. "Margaret Mitchell—*Gone with the Wind*—Source of the Title—GWTW." Awesome Stories, May 13. https://www.awesomestories.com/asset/view/SOURCE-of-the-TITLE-GWTW-Margaret-Mitchell-Gone-with-the-Wind.

Bragg, Georgia. 2012. *How They Croaked: The Awful Ends of the Awfully Famous*. New York: Bloomsbury.

Brooks, David. 2016. "The Power of a Dinner Table," *New York Times*, Oct. 18. http://nyti.ms/2u03GFF.

Brown, Peter. 2016. *The Wild Robot*. New York: Little, Brown.

Bush, Barbara, and Jenna Bush Hager. 2017. "The Bush Sisters Wrote the Obama Girls a Letter." *Time*, January 12. http://time.com/4632036/bush -sisters-obama-sisters/.

Caine, Karen. 2008. *Writing to Persuade*. Portsmouth, NH: Heinemann.

Carr, Teresa. 2017. "Off-Label Use: Should Drugs Do Double Duty?" *Consumer Reports*, January 4. www.consumerreports.org/drugs/off-label-use-should -drugs-do-double-duty/.

Carroll, Jon. 2006. "Failure Is a Good Thing." *This I Believe*, October 9. http:// thisibelieve.org/essay/23043/.

Chappell, Bill. 2016. "'He Will Be Our Brother': Boy, 6, Asks Obama to Bring Syrian Boy to Live with Him." NPR, *The Two Way*, September 22. www .npr.org/sections/thetwo-way/2016/09/22/495021467/he-will-be-our-brother -boy-6-asks-obama-to-bring-syrian-boy-to-live-with-him.

Clements, Andrew. 2014. "Where Did the Idea for *Frindle* Come From?" www .andrewclements.com/books-frindle-faq1.html.

Codell, Esmé Raji. 2003. *How to Get Your Child to Love Reading*. New York: Algonquin Books.

Coleman, Sarah E. 2017. "Get Over It!" *Young Rider*, January/February: 26–29.

Culham, Ruth. 2016. *The Writing Thief: Using Mentor Texts to Teach the Craft of Writing*. Portland, ME: Stenhouse.

Cullinan, Bernice E. 1995. *A Jar of Tiny Stars: Poems by NCTE Award–Winning Poets*. Honesdale, PA: Wordsong.

Cummings, Phil. 2016. *Newspaper Hats*. Illustrated by Owen Swan. Watertown, MA: Charlesbridge.

d'Avila-Latourrette, Victor-Antoine. 1989. *Twelve Months of Monastery Soups*. New York: Clarkson Potter.

Davies, Nicola. 2004. *Bat Loves the Night*. Illustrated by Sarah Fox-Davies. Boston: Candlewick Press.

———. 2005. *One Tiny Turtle*. Illustrated by Jane Chapman. Boston: Candle-wick Press.

Dictionary.com. 2017. s.v. "onomatopoeia." *Online Etymology Dictionary*. Doug-las Harper, historian. Accessed February 20. www.dictionary.com/browse /onomatopoeia.

Dotlich, Rebecca Kai. 1999. *What Is Square?* Illustrated by Maria Ferrari. New York: Scholastic.

Doubilet, David, and Jennifer Hayes. 2016. "The Caribbean's Crown Jewels." *National Geographic* November (5): 100–11.

Elder, Scott. 2017. "Penguin City." *National Geographic Kids*, February.

Foer, Joshua, Dylan Thuras, and Ella Morton. 2016. *Atlas Obscura: An Explorer's Guide to the World's Hidden Wonders*. New York: Workman Publishing.

Gaiman, Neil. 2008. *The Graveyard Book*. New York: HarperCollins.

Gibbons, Gail. 2001. *From Seed to Plant*. New York: Holiday House.

Graham, Bob. 2001. *"Let's Get a Pup!" Said Kate*. Boston: Candlewick Press.

Heard, Georgia. 1999. *Awakening the Heart: Exploring Poetry in Elementary and Middle School*. Portsmouth, NH: Heinemann.

Heffernan, Lisa. 2016. "Ready for College? Why Some Students Are Prepared More Than Others." NBC News online, March 4. www.nbcnews.com /feature/college-game-plan/ready-college-why-some-students-are-more -prepared-others-n531141.

Hickman, Steve. 2017. "A Time to Be Sad." *Mindful*, February.

Hinchman, Hannah. 1991. *A Life in Hand: Creating the Illuminated Journal*. Layton, UT: Peregrine Smith Books.

Holm, Jennifer L. 2014. *The Fourteenth Goldfish*. New York: Yearling.

Hood, Susan. 2016. *Ada's Violin: The Story of the Recycled Orchestra of Paraguay*. Illustrated by Sally Wern Comport. New York: Simon and Schuster Books for Young Readers.

Hoose, Phillip, and Hannah Hoose. 1998. *Hey, Little Ant*. Illustrated by Debbie Tilley. Berkeley, CA: Tricycle Press.

Hopkinson, Deborah. 2012. *Titanic: Voices from the Disaster*. New York: Scholastic Press.

Horn, Martha, and Mary Ellen Giacobbe. 2007. *Talking, Drawing, Writing: Lessons for Our Youngest Writers*. Portland, ME: Stenhouse.

Johnson, Angela. 2004. *Violet's Music*. Illustrated by Laura Huliska-Beith. New York: Dial Books.

Jones, Richard. 2002. "After Work." *The Writer's Almanac*, July 28. http:// writersalmanac.publicradio.org/index.php?date=2002/07/28.

Kenyon, Jane. 1996. "In the Nursing Home." In *Otherwise: New and Selected Poems*, 13. Saint Paul, MN: Graywolf Press.

Killgallon, Don, and Killgallon, Jenny. 2008. *Story Grammar for Elementary School: A Sentence Composing Approach*. Portsmouth, NH: Heinemann.

King, Martin Luther Jr. 1963. "Martin Luther King's Speech: 'I Have a Dream.'" Council on Foreign Relations, August 28. www.cfr.org/united-states/martin -luther-kings-speech-have-dream/p26070.

Kooser, Ted. 2009. "Splitting an Order." *The Writer's Almanac*, September 8. http://writersalmanac.publicradio.org/index.php?date=2009/09/08.

Krull, Kathleen. 2013. *Lives of the Scientists: Experiments, Explosions (and What the Neighbors Thought)*. Illustrated by Kathryn Hewitt. Boston: HMH Books for Young Readers.

Lane, Barry. 2008. *But How Do You Teach Writing?* New York: Scholastic Teaching Resources.

Latham, Irene. 2017. "ArtSpeak!," *Live Your Poem* (blog). Accessed February 23. http://irenelatham.blogspot.com/p/artspeak.html.

Louv, Richard. 2005. *Last Child in the Woods: Saving Our Children from Nature-Deficit Disorder*. New York: Algonquin.

Ludwig, Trudy. 2013. *The Invisible Boy*. Illustrated by Patrice Barton. New York: Knopf Books for Young Readers.

Mandell, Arlene. 2001. "Little Girl Grown." In *Mothers and Daughters: A Poetry Celebration*, edited by June Cotner, 107. New York: Crown.

Millay, Edna St. Vincent. 1981. *Edna St. Vincent Millay Collected Lyrics*, 75. New York: Harper Colophon Books.

Mitchell, Margaret. 1936. *Gone with the Wind*. New York: Macmillan.

Murray, Donald M. 1990. *Shoptalk: Learning to Write with Writers*. Portsmouth, NH: Heinemann.

Newkirk, Thomas. 2014. *Minds Made for Stories: How We Really Read and Write Informational and Persuasive Texts*. Portsmouth, NH: Heinemann.

Niven, Jennifer. 2016. *All the Bright Places*. New York: Ember.

Noland, Sudie Bond. 2011. "The True Value of Life." *This I Believe*, December 9. http://thisibelieve.org/essay/30261/.

NY Book Editors. 2016. "All About Point of View: Which One Should You Use?" Accessed February 20, 2017. http://nybookeditors.com/2016/01/all -about-point-of-view-which-one-should-you-use/.

Park, Barbara. 1996. *Mick Harte Was Here*. New York: Yearling.

Parsons, Stephanie. 2005. *First Grade Writers*. Portsmouth, NH: Heinemann.

Paterson, Katherine. 1977. *Bridge to Terabithia*. New York: Thomas Y. Crowell.

Paul, Miranda. 2015. *Water Is Water: A Book About the Water Cycle*. Illustrated by Jason Chin. New York: Roaring Brook Press.

Philipps, Dave. 2017. "Troops Who Cleaned Up Radioactive Islands Can't Get Medical Care." *New York Times*, January 28.

Pinkney, Andrea Davis. 2002. *Ella Fitzgerald: The Tale of a Vocal Virtuosa*. Illustrated by Brian Pinkney. New York: Jump at the Sun.

Pipher, Mary. 2007. *Writing to Change the World*. New York: Riverhead Books.

Pitts, Leonard. 2000. "A Letter to His Son on His 18th Birthday." *Orlando Sentinel*, July 8. http://articles.orlandosentinel.com/2000-07-18/news/0007180096 _1_18th-birthday-staring-backup-plan.

Portalupi, JoAnn, and Ralph Fletcher. 2004. *Teaching the Qualities of Writing*. Portsmouth, NH: Heinemann.

Preston, Elizabeth. 2016. "Nosy News: A Fish with an Eye for Faces." *Ask*, November/December: 3.

Ray, Katie Wood. 1999. *Wondrous Words: Writers and Writing in the Elementary Classroom*. Urbana, IL: NCTE.

———. 2002. *What You Know By Heart: How to Develop Curriculum for Your Writing Workshop*. Portsmouth, NH: Heinemann.

———. 2006. *Study Driven: A Framework for Planning Units of Study in the Writing Workshop*. Portsmouth, NH: Heinemann.

Ray, Mary Lyn. 2004. *Welcome, Brown Bird*. Illustrated by Peter Sylvada. New York: Harcourt.

Robertson, Michelle. 2015. "Recovery Season." *Orion Magazine*. https://orion magazine.org/article/recovery-season/.

Rosemond, John. 2016. "In a Family, Parents' Relationship Comes First." www .rosemond.com/December-2016.html.

Ruurs, Margriet. 2016. *Stepping Stones: A Refugee Family's Journey*. Illustrated by Nizar Ali Badr. Translated by Falah Raheem. Victoria, BC: Orca.

Ruzzo, Karen, and Mary Anne Sacco. 2004. *Significant Studies for Second Grade: Reading and Writing Investigations for Children*. Portsmouth, NH: Heinemann.

Schreiber, Anne. 2010. *Pandas*. Washington, DC: National Geographic Children's Books.

Sheinkin, Steve. 2012. *Bomb: The Race to Build—and Steal—the World's Most Dangerous Weapon*. New York: Flashpoint.

Shen, Lily. 2011. "Beware the Squirrelstein." *Complaint Box* (blog), *New York Times*, November 21. https://cityroom.blogs.nytimes.com/2011/11/21 /complaint-box-beware-the-squirrelstein/?_r=0.

Simon, Seymour. 1995. *Sharks*. New York: HarperCollins.

Surowiecki, James. 2017. "Where the Second Avenue Subway Went Wrong." *New Yorker*, January 23. www.newyorker.com/magazine/2017/01/23/where -the-second-avenue-subway-went-wrong.

Taylor, Mildred D. 1976. *Roll of Thunder, Hear My Cry*. New York: Dial Press.

VanDerwater, Amy Ludwig. 2007. "Once a Squirrel, Always a Squirrel." WBFO, Buffalo's NPR News Station, April 21. http://news.wbfo.org/post/listener -commentary-once-squirrel-always-squirrel-0.

———. 2013. *Forest Has a Song*. New York: Clarion.

White, E. B. 1952. *Charlotte's Web*. New York: HarperCollins.

Woodson, Jacqueline. 2012. *Each Kindness*. Illustrated by E. B. Lewis. New York: Nancy Paulsen Books.

"Cabin of One Hundred Lights" by Rebecca Kai Dotlich. Copyright © 2018 by Rebecca Kai Dotlich. Used with permission from Curtis Brown, Ltd., and the author.

"Brave" by Sara Holbrook. Copyright © 2018 by Sara Holbrook. Used with permission from the author.

"Little Cat" by Lesléa Newman. Copyright © 2018 by Lesléa Newman. Used with permission from Curtis Brown, Ltd., and the author.

"Pen, Not an Ordinary Object" by F. Isabel Campoy. Copyright © 2018 by F. Isabel Campoy. Used with permission from the author.

"One Day" by Renée M. LaTulippe. Copyright © 2018 by Renée M. LaTulippe. Used with permission from the author.

"Putting in the Work" by Charles Waters. Copyright © 2018 by Charles Waters. Used with permission from Stimola Literary Studio and the author.

Chapter 6 Poems

"One Blue Door" by Pat Mora. Copyright © 2002 by Pat Mora. Originally published in *This Big Sky*. New York, NY: Scholastic Inc. Reprinted with permission from Curtis Brown, Ltd., and the author.

"When I Open the Door" by Naomi Shihab Nye. Copyright © 2018 by Naomi Shihab Nye. Used with permission from the author.

"The Lion at the Door" by Juanita Havill. Copyright © 2018 by Juanita Havill. Used with permission from the author.

Afterword Poem

"As" by Lee Bennett Hopkins. Copyright © 2018 by Lee Bennett Hopkins. Used with permission from Curtis Brown, Ltd., and the author.